Peyton Pitt

Desperate Destruction

PEYTON PITT

WESTBOW°
PRESS
A DIVISION OF THOMAS NELSON
& ZONDERVAN

Scripture taken from the Holy Bible, NEW INTERNATIONAL VERSION®. Copyright © 1973, 1978, 1984 by Biblica, Inc. All rights reserved worldwide. Used by permission. NEW INTERNATIONAL VERSION® and NIV® are registered trademarks of Biblica, Inc. Use of either trademark for the offering of goods or services requires the prior written consent of Biblica US, Inc.

WestBow Press books may be ordered through booksellers or by contacting:

WestBow Press
A Division of Thomas Nelson & Zondervan
1663 Liberty Drive
Bloomington, IN 47403
www.westbowpress.com
1 (866) 928-1240

Because of the dynamic nature of the Internet, any web addresses or links contained in this book may have changed since publication and may no longer be valid. The views expressed in this work are solely those of the author and do not necessarily reflect the views of the publisher, and the publisher hereby disclaims any responsibility for them.

Any people depicted in stock imagery provided by Thinkstock are models, and such images are being used for illustrative purposes only. Certain stock imagery © Thinkstock.

ISBN: 978-1-4908-5573-8 (sc)
ISBN: 978-1-4908-5574-5 (e)

Library of Congress Control Number: 2014918117

Printed in the United States of America.

WestBow Press rev. date: 10/28/2014

Contents

This is a true story. The names have been changed to protect all family members and friends who have journeyed through these events along side me. Please understand, I am not trained medically, and I have no education in psychology. The facts included throughout this book are life lessons. They have been learned the hard way, at the expense of the people I love and wanted to protect. I cannot say you will have the same outcome. The people I have met seem to have identical lifestyles and repeat the cycle of lies and hurt, especially to the people that love them most. I pray that something in this story will help you decide to do something different, change your actions in a positive way, and recognize that God can help you. I chose the title for this book carefully. By the time I realized how addicted my son was to drugs, he had become desperate. It was at this point I realized his controlling need had destroyed family, friends and would soon destroy his life.

Peyton Pitt

1

Before I formed you in the womb I knew you
Jeremiah 1:5

This is a story of heartache and pain that could have and should have been avoided. I placed a high priority on the relationship I had with my children. I worked hard to make sure they received the love and attention that children desire. The parental attitude we displayed was to be involved in the activities the children displayed interest. My husband coached little league baseball for our oldest son. The close proximity of the ages required our sons to play baseball many times at the same exact time. As they grew, their interest was in church activities and classes in school that came with a privilege of traveling for competion in other states. Although many times this was expensive, we made sure they could be a part of a class they desired and we felt the opportunity for them was irreplaceable. After my husband stopped coaching, we were the parents at every ball game. We went to parent-teacher conferences. When our children had a performance, whether school or church related I never missed it. So I will be candid and tell you this is not how I thought my relationship with my child would progress.

God is never surprised by the events in our life. If I had any thought that our lives would have taken this direction, I would have made reservations for heaven right then, and asked God to take me now. This has been the most difficult life anyone could ever imagine and the purpose I have in telling this story is to keep someone else from making the same mistakes and facing the same heartache and hardships that my family has.

My grandmother was my example for Christian faith. I grew up in her care while my parents worked. She spent her time reading the Word of God, cooking and sewing. This is an amazing fact because there would be days she would have seven or more grandchildren in her care. Discipline was spoken, because we knew to respect any request, she made. Her personality was soft-spoken and without question all that knew her desired obedience. It was my desire to have a faith and personality like her. I did not get her soft-spoken style; I talk so much more than she ever did and as for her steadfast faith, I am still trying to achieve the level she maintained.

At the age of fifteen, my father found out he would need heart surgery. Without his income, my family really struggled, and as soon as possible I went to work. The school provided a class that gave you school credits for working so I attended school until lunch and worked each afternoon. I knew college was not an option, so I prayed that God would find a man for me that loved God as much as I did. God answered my prayer. We met and married within a year without debt. We have been married over thirty years. We put off marriage to make sure we had all the things we needed for our home. We wanted those things paid for before we were married.

One of the discussions we had before we married was about disagreements. In his home, his mother was vocal. Because of the anger in his home when he was younger, he really did not want children. However, he knew I did, and it was agreed our home would not at any time be a battlefield. We made a promise we would not for a moment fight in front of our children. Our two boys will tell you, we kept that promise. Growing up they knew we disagreed, but we never fought. Not while they were both living at home.

> ***For I know the plans I have for you," declares the Lord, "plans to prosper you and not to harm you, plans to give you hope and a future.***
>
> ***Jeremiah. 29:11***

God had plans for me. The biggest problem was I was involved in the plan. My husband attended church about two years. One Sunday night he thought he was having a heart attack and going to die. I wanted him to go to the hospital, but he refused. He went to the doctor, and it turned out to be anxiety attacks. We have battled these for many years. When I say we, my husband takes issue with this because in his own words, I do not understand what he feels. Nevertheless, these attacks truly cost us years of living, so in my mind it affected us both. Why don't we follow God's plans? When we are young, instead of relying on God and working through the stress, we just give up and give in. Now that I am older and wiser, I can genuinely understand why God never gives us anymore than just a moment at a time. If we knew what was coming we would really destroy the lives of family, friends and strangers.

God knows our knowledge and wisdom is not enough to deal with the situations we face each day. God sees the beginning and the end; we see only the now. That was the situation we were in. The truth is, no one really wants to deal with what is taking place today. Discussing yesterday was easy. There was always a great plan and knowledge, but it is gone and everyone has an excuse for the reason things turned out the way they did. Generally, everyone wants to blame someone else for his or her mistakes and problems. Tomorrow has not gotten here so you can say all these things you will do, and you are thinking about. But what excuse do you have for today? You have no excuse. The problem is if you face the fact you have a problem, then you may have to do something about your issue. No one wants to talk about it, or even think about it. It is your responsibility and there is no one to blame but you. To help with my husband's anxiety, I thought we should have a baby. That is funny now, but I thought it would help. I told you when you get older you get wiser. Seven years and fertility drugs were finally how pregnancy happened. We started the drugs in January and the doctor, who was a friend, told me (in December) if you don't get pregnant this month you will need to go to a hospital in a larger city, and you will have several children at once. I got pregnant that month. The change in the hormones made me so sick. I lost thirty pounds and was hospitalized eight times because I was dehydrated. I remember being in the bed unable to cry any tears because l had no fluids left in my body. Two sweet nurses sat with me, and I was holding my stomach and promising God if he protected this baby, I would give this child to Him. The sickness lasted the whole time. Three weeks early but very healthy, a beautiful baby boy (Bruiser) was born. No two parents could have been more proud.

I took him to church by myself. He loved going, and he was independent. He dressed himself and I would allow him to go just like he wanted. Many times he went to church in cowboy boots and shorts. The elderly couples adored him. He was a real talker, and they would pat his head and tell him how well he looked. This fueled his determination to do things on his own. He paid close attention to adults. One week the preacher was speaking and with his cowboy boots scraping against the wood as he tried to stand, (he was about three) he got onto his feet and shouted, "I can't hear what you're telling me!" Sometimes after that, from the pulpit before service would start the pastor would ask, "Bruiser can you hear me?" Bruiser would answer truthfully from his seat.

Then it happened; I got sick. The only time I ever do is if I am pregnant. I called the doctor, and he told me to come to his office. I was pregnant! No fertility drugs this time and I feel like God has given us a great gift and a huge surprise. God's ways are not always the same way as ours. We had to plan and work so hard to have the first child, and this was just a blessing. I experienced the same sickness, and again I make the same promises to God. However, this time I feel assurance about this child, he was already a gift from my Heavenly Father, therefore dedicating him to God seemed so natural. I promise God that this child will belong to Him, and I will do my best to raise them both right. Because of the continued nausea, there is an underlying fear that something could be wrong. There was never a need to worry.

> *Consider it pure joy, my brothers and sisters, whenever you face trials of many kinds, because you know that the testing of your faith produces perseverance. Let perseverance finish its work so that you may be mature and complete, not lacking anything.*
>
> *James 1:2-4*

Have you ever considered your curses and blessings? As you read further this thought will return to you. God knew all along the path chosen, but there was another way. The complete faith was available for everyone included in this family, not just one. It's hard to remember a lot of joy during so much pain. There is no happiness when the people you love are hurting. But God sees the end from the beginning. We don't have that ability. We never will.

2

They disciplined us for a little while as they thought best; but God disciplines us for our good, in order that we may share in his holiness.

Hebrews 12:10

God has plans, and those plans can only be known if we are in His Word. When we had Buster that was where my refining began. I promised God that our children would be raised to love Him. Because of my husband's anxiety, the children and I attend church without him. The children are involved in baseball; their Dad attends these games, and we never miss them. Many times we are the only two parents in attendance. This has had a lifetime impact on our sons. The children and I attend church, and everything appears normal and happy. This is life for most people. By appearance, what do you see? Are things really what they seem to be? In homes, where families argue and disagree and it eventually progresses to a level of abuse, children are powerless. Addictions sometimes begin because of pain from abuse and other times from desire to forget what is happening in the situations they are living. The children of the addicts are repeating the behavior they have witnessed. Physical violence is prevalent throughout our society and women often leave, but they return once the abuser apologizes. Usually, this cycle repeats again and again. Life is strange; you just keep going through the motions, and God does what He must to get us to listen. We are not always happy in our life, but God is always speaking if we listen. Obedience is a choice but we usually choose to disobey. So life keeps changing, and God keeps trying to get our attention.

In our home, the children continue to grow up and suddenly God gets my attention. I had what I thought was pleurisy and had to go into the emergency room. That one trip changed my life. I was sent to a larger city to be diagnosed with an Autoimmune Disease. This disease over the years has destroyed much of my life, and stress exacerbates the symptoms. However, God was faithful, just like my grandmother taught me. Depend on God; He will see you through everything.

Remember, college was not an option. The first good job I had was at a grocery store. Every Friday night, I had a customer who worked in a bank, and he encouraged me on numerous occasions to come into the bank and put in an application. After I graduated, I was in town one day, not prepared to apply for any jobs much less have an interview. I had just turned eighteen and wisdom was not my greatest gift at this time, but God can use the foolishness of a young girl and turn it into a success for Him in the years to come. I got hired right that moment. I started Monday morning at the bank and worked nights my last two weeks at the grocery. I learned everything I could at the bank, starting with keying and filing checks. After about six months, I became a teller. Several years pass and God was faithful. I received another promotion, this time in a supervisor position. The bank built a new office in the same city, and I was moved to that location. I maintained that identical position for several years. In large banks, there are Regional Executive's that are moved into positions from other parts throughout the country. Our Banking

Center had a new man from the south, and he decided to transfer me to a neighboring county, as a supervisor. This was a challenging situation. I was completing tasks as a Manager, although I did not have that title. I was not given Banking Center manager title for three months. I was not from the community and did not know the history of the Banking Center. This was a small town, and I was an outsider. When you are new to a Banking Center, the towns people do not like for outsiders to come into their towns and work, so I was scrutinized for many things. People want to know who you are and where you're from. Really the same things most people want to know when you meet anyone new. While I worked there the office was robbed. Bear in mind, my husband is having anxiety attacks. I cannot add to his stress with my work issues. At this time, I was getting into my car, turning on preaching and praise music, praying the whole way to work. The truth is my relationship with God strengthened so much. Before I left the Banking Center, I had to disband the board of directors. If you really want to be unpopular in a community, this is the way to do it. Tell a whole group of leaders within the community they are not needed and no longer have a voice in the bank they had founded years earlier.

> *When I was in distress, I sought the Lord; at night I stretched out untiring hands, and I would not be comforted.*
>
> *Psalms 77: 2*

I am weary and because of this overwhelming feeling, there are times it causes me to remain in stubbornness and refuse comfort. God is the only one that can provide real peace and comfort to anyone. However, I have to want the things God gives every day.

Nevertheless, all too often we are so wrapped up in the trouble, we can't break the bonds long enough to see he has his arms outstretched to save us all the time.

After three years, I was transferred back to the location that I had previously been only a supervisor. I was happy under the circumstances. When you have been through all the situations that I have encountered, you recognize an opportunity and feel blessed when you receive it. Things are never perfect in any world. Knowledge and growth come through difficulty. I endured another robbery, theft by employees and overall issues that all managers are required to face daily that ultimately became a quarter century legacy. God allowed me to become a Vice President. I had no college degree. I did not deserve what I was given, I was grateful. God was faithful when things were hard, and yet I felt so alone. In my mind, I thought things just could not get any worse. Please hear me when I tell you this. Never hear or believe that lie from Satan. Things can and will get worse. From this point on, my prayer is that you will hear my heart. I love my family, and most of all I love Buster. Love is not all about taking, and my son is giving nothing, but he is expecting everything.

God gave up His Son for us and all He requires of us is to Love His Son with our whole heart, our mind and with all our strength and to have a relationship with Him. Relationship requires giving, not taking all the time. I feel sure God, being our Heavenly Father wonders how much more we, as His children can ask for and what else can we need?

3

The righteous person may have many troubles, but the Lord delivers him from them all;

Psalms 34:19

My husband left an Assistant Manager Job to work at a factory, so he would not have to meet people. He continued to go to ball games and school functions, but there were many times that he could not attend events due to the anxiety. Both boys question him endlessly about his lack of participation at some gatherings. Anxiety is impossible to explain to grade-school children. This causes him to feel even worse. My disease started with several lesions on my lungs that initially looked like Hodgkin's (a type of cancer) but the autoimmune disease I have is taking control over many parts of the body. Over the years, I continued to do all the things with the children I could. For the most part, I don't recall any event either child was denied because a parent could not attend.

At church, I taught children's church in front of the congregation each Sunday, and I loved doing it. Both the boys loved church. When my oldest was in the fifth grade, there was an issue at church. The pastor said that children's church took too long, and I needed to cut it back from two minutes down to one minute. We had about twenty children affected. A lot of the adults loved this time and were very pleased with this part of the service. The next week I amended it to one minute and made sure someone timed it, so I did not exceed my allotted time. The pastor told me I still used too much time, and he needed to eliminate this portion of the service. I accepted that. It hurt me, but it hurt the parents too. There were other things I could see happening from the vantage point of the choir loft and it was destroying my faith in the pastor. Not my faith in God. Finally, I just couldn't go into that church anymore. However, this one choice was the utter destruction of my sons. My oldest son was friends with what most people, would call all the right people. You know the kid's with swimming pools, and their fathers were CEOs of companies. Remember I am a Vice President, but we live in a 1,000 square foot house and stay there because of my disease. My husband and I don't want to be foolish about going into debt.

I came home for lunch one day, and found Bruiser with marijuana in our living room. This is the first time I saw my son do anything like this in his whole life. It is devastating. I had a discussion with both boys and explained that some family members were alcoholics and could not control their addictions. They could be the one that would try something one time and cannot stop. That person turned out to be my youngest son, Buster. He began smoking at ten. My husband and I did not know. Pretending often turns into the actions themselves. Pay attention to the actions of your children. Do they pretend to smoke or have anger issues and mistreat another person? If they are old enough to pretend, then you can have the conversation it is wrong. Buster always loved cologne and he sprayed plenty, but I know now it was to disguise the tobacco smell. It is not cute for children to act like they are smoking.

My mother in law kept the boys while I worked, with all my nephews (three) and nieces (one). She had six kids every day all about two years apart. So watching this one child was impossible. I never intended for her to watch my children. I enrolled Bruiser in daycare. The next day I went to pick him up, and there she was in a rocker with him in her arms. She had applied for a job and went to work that morning. I just gave up and let her keep him at home, so when the others were born she wanted to keep them all. However, remember I talked to both the boys about drinking and smoking and never starting something because you might not be able to stop.

Even at ten, children feel that parents do not know or understand how they feel. Children think you do not understand what you are talking about or what they are going through. I teach fifth graders in Sunday school, and it's amazing what they will tell me, but would never tell their parents. Some children believe that if they tell someone about Jesus, they will be in trouble, because they cannot say Jesus's name at school. Some also believe that their parents will be furious because they told another person about Jesus. They know that their parents will be annoyed about any problem at school. They don't doubt they would know what to say, they just don't want to cause any problems. Even if the child they are with daily may never be told about Jesus, they will not tell because of the consequences at home. This gets better when they get older, and then they really don't worry so much about pleasing parents. The pressure is very high as a child, which is why they gravitate toward gangs and get involved in activities that parents would never approve of. The deception for them is done by older children who use and abuse through torment and just meanness. Even so, as the kids get older this too changes.

Do not deceive yourselves. If any of you think you are wise by the standards of this age, you should become "fools" so that you may become wise. For

> **the wisdom of this world is foolishness in God's**
> **sight. As it is written: "He catches the wise in their**
> **craftiness"**
>
> **1 Corinthians 3:18-19**

The thing with deception is Buster deceived us for a long time, and it cost us a lot, but God was never deceived. And the thing is when you get by with deception, when it works out it gets bigger and bigger so Buster just allowed his foolishness to grow. Remember I had the conversation with my sons about addictions. My oldest son was not innocent. He drank and smoked. He has felt guilt that somehow he was responsible for his brother ending up an addict. Buster freely admits that his brother begged him not to smoke marijuana. When Buster smoked it the first time he could not feel his face, he said he hit his face over and over and it had no feeling, even though others were with them, Buster said his brother cried and begged him to stop and never do it again. Buster can't just stop anything; he has an addictive personality; he moves from one thing to another. He moved to drinking and finally pills. As a parent, you think you know what your child is doing. When they are teenagers you take precautions to protect "them." When they would go to homes of people I knew, they would call and let us know they were there, this was to relieve us from the worry of bad behavior. I trusted these families, but they allowed teenagers to drink and do drugs in their homes. Some adults believe that if they allow supervised drinking, it protects the children. I will be the first person to tell you; my child cannot accept one drink. He has to have all of them and then wants more. How can some people just stop drinking? Why do some people have to go get help? What if I offered drinks to kids who became alcoholics?

Every fall a friend of the boys has a cookout. This is out in the country on a farm, and both boys liked to go. Food and alcohol were provided. My boys were fourteen and sixteen when they started going. The course of lives can be changed because people offer something to children who legally could not obtain it for years. If I had known that alcohol was part of the plans for the overnight cookout our children would not have been given permission to go. This would have caused problems between the boys and us, but they knew when they went that we would never approve. God requires obedience from each one of us. In this case, what good has come from this? God did not call us to be friends to our children, but to lead them. Will we know the result of our behavior?

> *So then, each of us will give an account of ourselves to God. Therefore let us stop passing judgment on one another. Instead, make up your mind not to put any stumbling block or obstacle in the way of a brother or sister.*
>
> *Romans 14:12-13*

We don't like to think about giving an account for the past. Who have we influenced? Do the choices I make lead others to Christ or do I embarrass God by the life I live? In the case of children and teenagers, these may be life-altering decisions. The future is fragile, and some things can never be restored; God will be asking what each one has done. Do you have an answer?

4

Jesus said to him, 'You shall love the LORD your God with all your heart, with all your soul, with all with all your mind.' This is the first and great commandment. And the second is like it: 'You shall love your neighbor as yourself.'

Matthew 22:37–39

Love takes on many forms. I wanted my children so much. I went into the hospital and promised God I would give them to Him. The problem with that was they decided something entirely different. My father was so proud of our boys; he was coming into our house every day to see them. He gave them both a dip of tobacco. He loved to take them riding about the country and look at cows. He called the cows his honeys and the boys thought that was so much fun. I tell you again, God knows all things and works it out without consulting us because we would make a mess out of it. I was at work a lot of times so it wasn't about seeing me. Dad was scheduled for surgery on his heart again, but first they needed to take out his spleen; this was supposed to be minor surgery. He never made it home. He had surgery on Tuesday and died on Thursday night around midnight. I knew the moment he died. Sitting downstairs in the waiting room, I felt that something was wrong. I went through the ICU floor and was met by a nurse and promptly told I could not go down that hall. I explained that I had to, because I knew that my father was dying right that moment. In seconds, a chaplain appeared and asked mother and I to go in an office, and he told us that my father had died. I knew he had, but I wanted to see him. It was peaceful. All the tubes and machines were gone, and he was not suffering any more. It happened at midnight, and by the time I got into the car it was around three. I drove home with all the windows down, radio up and sang hymns. I cried and laughed all at the same time. I cried because he won't see the boy's grow up, and because I will miss him. I laughed because he is free, from pain, pills and doctors. Bruiser plays one of his guitars. My dad would have been so happy about that. Dad sang and wrote songs and played with other guys all the time. Sometimes I am so overwhelmed by it; I cry until I have no more tears. Then laugh because he would have killed me because of Buster.

My mother and I went to arrange for Dad's funeral service, neither of my brother's felt like they could come and help. The next day I made it through the visitation without a tear, when it came time for the service itself, we played a recording of Dad singing gospel songs, and I did fine through that. However, as soon as the dirt was placed upon the casket I remember thinking I would die inside, and that's when my tears started. That was in November. Thanksgiving and Christmas that year just could not be celebrated. His death being around the holidays changed the way we attended all family events. With death, sadness can be overwhelming to everyone. The boys loved him and I was grieving, there was a change in behavior and since my husband, and I were working as well as the grieving; discipline was not meted out in a high measure.

Both the boys knew my stand on drinking and drugs. This was clear and stated whenever I found anything in my oldest son's things that caused me pain. Nevertheless, the truth was Buster was doing the same thing; he was just devious. Buster was selling drugs to kids and adults, and some of his customers were people we knew.

All that I was raised to believe, my faith; all that I had promised to God when I gave birth to both boys is absolutely a lie. My son is just a common drug dealer. I cannot put into words how devastated I am. (This information was recently disclosed to me.)

Bruiser was taking punishment sometimes for things that Buster had done. Buster was so crafty, yet we did not understand how bad he was. Buster sold drugs to people that should have told us what was going on. However, that would have exposed them. The worst thing we ever did was purchasing Buster a cell phone. He was on his phone constantly. One day, I was asked if his ear was the same shape as a phone.

In middle school, Buster was always the escort for the attendants during football homecoming. Even so, now that he has gotten so deep into this lifestyle, he is no longer interested in school functions. He still has girls around him, but I realize now they were doing the same things he was. He had to have certain jeans, shirts, shoes and hats. He always wanted to look nice. We were buying these things and find out years later he had money of his own. He had money but he did not earn that money; his money was filthy as far as I was concerned. His phone was his lifeline. To this day, he deletes everything. If someone calls our home, he deletes the number. It is a habit straight from deception. Lies just pour from his mouth. He never blinks. Tears can be turned on like a waterfall.

If you are a parent, these are things you cannot trust. Checking the history on the phone itself will not work. Go online and look up history for the cell phone. Be prepared when you get phone numbers; they use burn phones and can't be traced. Tears and "I promise" mean nothing. When searching cars and rooms, you need to be more creative than they are. Drugs can be in shoes, pockets of shirts, drawers lifted out and taped behind or under and so many more I can't list. The more devious they are and the longer they stay on drugs the craftier they become. In the attic, under the house became favorite hiding places. I know you think that your child would do none of these things. I pray you are right. I prayed so hard! This is like a nightmare that has no end; you want to wake up, but you don't know what to do or how to make it stop! Keep your mind open, love can be so blind; you never want to think your child would lie or steal, much less use drugs. As a parent, you taught your child right from wrong. They would never hurt me this way.

> *On the first day of the week we came together to break bread. Paul spoke to the people and, because he intended to leave the next day, kept on talking until midnight. There were many lamps in the upstairs room where we were meeting. Seated in a window was a young man named Eutychus, who was sinking into a deep sleep as Paul talked on and on. When he was sound asleep, he fell to the ground from the third story and was picked up dead. Paul went down, threw himself on the young man and put his arms around him. "Don't be alarmed," he said. "He's alive!" Then he went upstairs again and broke bread and ate. After talking until daylight, he left the people took the young man home alive and were greatly comforted.*
>
> *Acts 20:7-12*

I doubt when this happened to Paul, he would have ever thought that a person would have used an example such as this, but this is the only way I can try to make you understand. I was listening to God's Word; I was involved in Study and trying my best to be the example, but at some point I fell asleep and fell out. God had to focus me completely on Him. Would I have chosen this way? Never! I thought I was doing all I could to have a real relationship, but He knew there was something missing and focus on Him must be number one. But in no way is this over, I am at the start of this battle. I did not find this out for a long time, and it sickens me to know I had a drug dealer living in my home. Except, I knew something was going on!

At Buster's graduation, he wanted us to meet a girl he had been seeing. At this point, we still were unaware of his lifestyle, and we wanted the best for him. It wasn't long before he said that she was pregnant. He had no intention of marrying her. They had a wonderful baby boy. There exists no grandson in the world that is more handsome and precious to us. However, there have been times this child has been used as a weapon to get what is desired. One day, his girlfriend made the statement (in a fit of anger) he could not see his son, and Buster hit the deck with his fist. This is never a wise thing for anyone to do. He got a boxer's break. He refused to go to the hospital within a timely manner and when he went, it was too late to set the small bones; therefore, the hand swells every time he does much of anything with it. Except it started a relationship with pain pills he could not control. When this happened, he was working and had kept a job for years. At the time, the three lived together in apartment. This was temporary. They attempted to live together several times. The three of them, as a family is not the greatest situation for our grandson. Tempers and drug addiction is not an appropriate home life for a young child. One day, a girl Buster worked with showed him how to grind the pills down to snort them and how much quicker they would work. She also introduced him to a drug that took complete control over his life and absolutely destroyed every relationship he had. By the time he confessed to me, he was so addicted to this drug he has never to this day revealed the amount of money he owed to various dealers. I did research, and kids were dying because of this drug. He finally took a layoff and lay down to do nothing. He got pneumonia and was hospitalized for a lengthy time. He has a scar on his lung, and lost his job permanently but his love for the pills did not stop. He moved back home after that.

Do you remember being a young adult and thinking your parents were stupid? Children believe you are trying to destroy their total happiness ...they believe we are out of touch with reality, that parents are just embarrassing! The desire kids have today is to manipulate you with anger, with temper tantrums, with entitlement to the point to make you feel as though you have failed completely as a parent. The demand to have possessions to satisfy happiness and show love is unsound. Constant desire for money as well as "stuff" was Buster's mentality. This reasoning is rampant in society, and many parents feel defeated when they are unable to meet this kind of demand.

> *A person may think their own ways are right but the*
> *Lord weighs the heart.*
>
> *Proverbs 21:2*

We all feel like we are doing the right thing even if all those around us tell us it is clearly wrong. As a parent, to refuse to allow your child to come to your home to live would have been wrong. I was not taught to do that. You do not leave people on their own, when you know they cannot take care of themselves. He had no job, no insurance, no money, and no place to live. It would have been wrong to tell him he could not come to our home to live when we have an empty bedroom for him to sleep and money enough to feed him. God tells us to take care of one another. At this time, I wanted him to be in our home, so I would know he was well taken care of. Mothers do this. We love our children. God loves us the same way.

I try to focus on how God loves us like children...when I desire things that I am not spiritually ready for God knows that. It is the same thing as a three-year-old loving the brand-new car, getting into it and sitting behind the wheel. They pretend to drive and make all the noises, stopping, starting and honking horns. You as the parent would never give them the keys no matter how cute and lovable that child is when they make believe. That is happening to many people spiritually. God can't answer our prayers; we have not matured enough to be trusted with any of the things we keep asking for. That is why parents as friends never work. Someone must be responsible. You may grow old enough to get the keys to a car in this world and with it comes responsibility. If you ignore the rules, you will face fines and penalties. Tickets that cost money, wrecks that could cost injury to you, and it could cause death to someone you love, because you cannot obey. Rules are never fun, but they have a purpose. God would never allow a three-year-old to drive. Maturity and responsibility grow together. What age are you in your spirit? Have you grown at all since you asked Jesus to be Lord of your life?

5

Trust in the Lord with all your heart and lean not on your own understanding; in all your ways submit to him, and he will make your paths straight

Proverbs 3:5-6

When you lie down, you will not be afraid; when you lie down, your sleep will be sweet Have no fear of sudden disaster or of the ruin that overtakes the wicked, for the Lord will be at your side and will keep your foot from being snared.

Proverbs 3:24-26

I had to trust that God was in total control. Fear disappeared. God is leading and I now begin walking. I applied for Disability and was approved on the phone interview during my first call. My neurologist said over the years he had been in practice this had never happened. I paid for long-term disability throughout my career in the bank. This is a vital source of income; I make about the same money as I did when I was working. (Without bonuses) God knew what was approaching, and His plan included me.

My sister in law suddenly started to miss work. She went back to bed after she got up and got dressed for work. She had headaches in the past, but now they were worse. Her personality changed as well. She was always cheerful but now things were really funny to her. She couldn't identify people by their names; she would laugh and say again and again, that she knew who they were. She was diagnosed with an aggressive brain tumor and died within months. My husband was devastated losing his sister. They worked and ate lunch together every day. Watching her die was so agonizing.

Her death destroyed my mother in law. She sat down in a chair and grieved herself to death. No one could comfort her. We reminded her she had two sons and grandchildren who loved her. She had two great grandkids but nothing helped her with her grief. That was her only daughter. Two sons weren't the same. She loved them both and she had two daughters in laws she loved too. Nevertheless, this was her daughter; she just couldn't overcome it. We loved her as much as possible. She just gave up living. It took several years and she ended up with Parkinson's, but she was never the same. At the very end, she was so fragile; all her family was with her except Bruiser. The Hospice nurses felt the end was very near; Bruiser wouldn't get off work until eleven o'clock, and no one felt she would make it that long. Everyone spent quiet time with her. At 11:02 Bruiser ran down the hall and closed the door to talk with his grandmother. She heard every word. He opened the door, and everyone went in to be with her. At 11:05 she met Jesus face to face. Isn't God wonderful! He loves us all so much; He made it possible for each child to tell a grandmother good-bye and for a grandmother to hear every word. Everyone she loved was in that room and had spent time with her, but she waited for her last grandson to come home before she relaxed enough to go to her eternal home. God is great and merciful. This is one of those times, if we had known how all this would have been we would have made another way to travel, and it would not have been the beautiful end that we all got to experience.

I was distracted from what was going on at home, so Buster was doing his own thing. I believed with all my heart, I had raised my children with truth and value, and they would be responsible. I believed that the love they had for me and their father would be enough, and they would never go so wrong to hurt us to the level that Buster has. What Buster has done has been hard on the whole family. We all want to see healing but Buster just will not change.

> *"But seek ye first the kingdom of God, and his righteousness; and all these things shall be added unto you."*
>
> *Matthew 6:33*

> *Woe to those who call evil good and good evil who put darkness for light and light for darkness who put bitter for sweet and sweet for bitter Woe to those who are wise in their own eyes and clever in their own sight.*
>
> *Isaiah 5:20-21*

Buster really thought he was clever. We placed confidence in our boys. I don't want to leave the impression, not to ever trust your children. If you see any transition that you cannot explain and your child has no excuse, if grades begin to decline, a lack of participation in school activities or family functions, this should be a warning to a parent something is amiss in your child. There will be changes in sleep patterns but when the lifestyle your child has embraced is new and one you do not approve then you need to get in your child's business. I don't mean to just ask questions I mean really nose around. The above scripture states, Woe to those...do you know what is woe? Grief or overwhelming sadness. People that make these choices never think this through. Grief and overwhelming sadness, does not come to them until much later in the process. The family it touches initially become calloused to the lies and tears and professed change that addicts promise constantly. God forgives as far as the east is to the west, but people are too human to have the capacity to forget this much pain. Sadness can dominate a person when this much deception and evil are consuming a person they love. It is overwhelming when you are helpless to stop the choices they continue to make.

Somewhere along the line Buster started seeking things of this world and God was not included. Destruction comes with this world and all those standing close are destroyed or getting injured in some way. We never think about who else we are hurting when we make selfish choices, but the one's you love suffer most.

6

If any of you lacks wisdom, you should ask God who gives generously to all without finding fault, and it will be given to you

James 1:5

Buster's addiction has grown to a need that he cannot pay for. He joined a gang to feed his habit. Most addicts lie. This is information that I am learning as time passes. Lying is just like taking the drugs, it is a habit that as the need arises, you fill it that moment and worry over the consequences later. The problem with lies, one leads to another and so forth. I learn this lesson in a very hard way.

A young man in our church (I just started one day going to church alone) needed a place to stay. I had told God I would never allow others to come into our home; it's far too small. This young man ended up sleeping on our couch. The fact is he robbed a small market and had been using cocaine. I was the one that had to go to the police department and identify him on the video. He has been living in our home for months and is loved by my grandson. Because he was living with us I knew where he was going many times and the police had asked for my help with his arrest. I did not want the arrest at my home because of my grandson. One morning he said he was going to pick up his mail at the post office, so I called the police to let them know where he would be, and they arrested him. The young man called me and asked "How can you say that's me on that video?"

I told him how hurt I was he would lie, and in moments all the truth came out. He confessed to the officers about the robbery. Months later, he went to prison. When you are confined to prison, you are required to submit a list of three names you want to have contact with while incarcerated. He included me as a person to call from prison. While he was there I sent him many sermons, letters and cards. I had no idea God was preparing me for what was coming with Buster.

Buster has tormented his father and me. One Sunday night he called and told me he was being held hostage, with a gun to his head. This went on for hours. As a parent can you imagine how you would feel, not knowing where your child is? When all this began I was sick and cried many nights and days over this. At one point, he asked for help, and I took him to meet five other young people that looked just like him. All of them nothing but skin and bones and they went into a detox place in a larger city. According to him, this re-hab cost us money too. The first mistake we ever made was giving him any money. I implore you from the bottom of my heart...DO NOT EVER give an addict any money for any reason. If there is a bill, you want to help with, go pay the debt yourself. If they need food, you purchase the food. Do not give a gift card, they trade that for drugs, cigarettes and most likely the food too, but if they die of starvation at least you tried to feed them.

> *You who practice deceit, your tongue plots destruction; it is like a sharpened razor.*
>
> *Psalms 52:2*

An addict can think of things you, and I would never consider. Buster has the most vivid imagination and can come up with endless heart-breaking stories, but after four years, I have allowed him to cause me to become unfeeling in some things. An addict has a reason for everything they do, and most are not logical. You cannot reason with someone that is not competent to take care of him or herself.

When it became clear I could no longer work, I had enough money to comfortably plan the rest of my life, not elaborately, but not having to worry constantly about groceries and utilities. No mortgage, no credit card debt or car payments. Over a four-year period, Buster has lied and manipulated us out of everything we had to live on. There were times we were told that guns were placed on my grandchild when Buster, and his girlfriend went to pick him up from pre-k. You may have done something different, and because I am giving you this information, I pray you will. Except I can, right this minute think of numerous people out of thousands of dollars because of the same circumstances. That is the reason I wrote this story. Not only have I lost all my savings I now have a mortgage and credit card debt. When you have good credit, and you think your child and grandchild might truly be in danger you do whatever it takes to protect them. I am so angry now that I realize the truth. Buster swears that all of it is the truth, and he has never lied, but I know some things for sure. He and my grandson's mother are not together, but recently, they spent the night at her mother's house. (He did not know we knew that) He called and whispered he had been kidnapped. We called to verify they were there, and YES they were! He is on the phone extorting money from us. When we saw him later that day, he said he shouldn't have done that. So you question all of it. We are talking about over two hundred thousand dollars. He has done the same thing to other people we know. He will call and pretend to be my husband, tells them we are on the way to take Buster out of town, and he won't ever be back. He is so deceitful. When you try to talk to him about it, he tells you that, somehow you don't understand what is going on and gets mad and leaves. He has no driver's license because of child support, and he won't work. The pain in your heart is first, and then comes anger and hurt. I have been to the police but because he lives in our home we can't just force him on the street we have to file papers and that takes 30 days. It is hard to put your child on the street in the cold without a car, without a job, without food or friends. His little boy will ask me if I will really do that to his daddy. My grandson is watching me and listening to see what I will do. This is so hard! The pain is unbearable, and you feel like you cannot win. If I had no grandson the answer would be so easy, I could send him to prison for what he has done.... But there is a little boy involved, his heart, his future. My grandson loves for his dad to give him a bath, they have bubbles everywhere. His dad sits with him to do his homework; these are memories that cannot be restored. How do I fix that? I get angry over what I have lost. Then I will have scripture go through my head and remember what Christ went through and I just can't do it. I can't give more money, there is nothing left to give. But now I am strong enough to tell him no. According to him, he has to pay to get out of the gang, or they will kill him. I finally don't want to hear the explanations anymore. I just beg him to go. His famous lines are.... give me one Last Chance. It made me think of Bartemaeus

As Jesus approached Jericho, a blind man was sitting by the roadside begging. When he heard the crowd going by, he asked what was happening. They told him, "Jesus of Nazareth is passing by." He called out, "Jesus, Son of David, have mercy on me!

Hose who led the way rebuked him and told him to be quiet, but he shouted all the more, "Son of David, have mercy on me!" Jesus stopped and ordered the man to be brought to him. When he came near, Jesus asked him, "What do you want me to do for you?" "Lord, I want to see," he replied. Jesus said to him, "Receive your sight; your faith has healed you." Immediately he received his sight and followed Jesus, praising God When all the people saw it, they all praised God.

Luke 18:35-43

Jesus chose that path he would travel. He was on his way to be crucified. If you did not see him on this road, you would not see him: this was the Last Chance anyone would have. He would be taken captive and killed soon. Bartemaeus heard the people talking about him coming up the road, and he made sure not to miss the opportunity. In the Scriptures, it says he called out Jesus name and asked for mercy. The people got onto him for it. But he got louder. He knew it was truly his Last Chance! Jesus asked what do you want? Jesus knows what we want.... but He always lets us maintain dignity, and He gives us grace. Bartemaeus wanted to see. Jesus gave him his sight back, because of his faith. What about my Faith and your Faith? What is it you want most of all? If Jesus were passing by you for the Last Time.... would He hear you shouting "JESUS" and if He heard you and asked you, "What do you want?" What would your answer be?

7

The righteous person may have many troubles but the Lord delivers him from them all;

Psalm 34:19

When I quit attending church, the boy's behavior began to decline. I did not perceive that until years later considering the hours I was working. To be a really good Manager I had to work fifty five to sixty five hours a week and there were lots of times I worked on Sunday. Banker's hours aren't what people have been led to believe in some movies. My oldest son went to college, but he did not apply himself except to drinking and smoking weed. While in college, he met people born in other religions. He felt that the God he loved would not allow people to die and go to hell because they did not get the same opportunity we all did. It troubled him, and he would not discuss it. It was an unreasonable discussion to have as far as he was concerned. Church was something he would not attend or discuss with me. Both boys have done things that went against the morals I had worked so hard to teach them, and it grieved me. Currently, since I am older, God reminds me all the time...now you know HOW I FEEL!

It never occurred to me until I got into all this distress that God must be crushed by our rejection and the lack of desire to receive the good things He has for us. All He wants is for us to do our best, and

His whole agenda is to keep as many people as possible from dying and going to hell. We make it so complicated.

My oldest has chosen a path I do not approve, he and his girlfriend live together. My children were taught to show honor and respect through the act of marriage. My youngest is a single father. His son stays in our home most days. Buster does not work so his child support is not current. His son usually goes to see his mom on Friday night (sometimes) and comes back on Saturdays. He is happy with us. We talk about many things. My grandson is wise beyond his years. His knowledge is worldly, but I try to instill in him about the love of God. He has seen things most adults have never seen. I wish I could change it for him. I cannot

Because of the tension, the home that we have vowed to never disagree has turned to a war zone. My grandson has heard me shout and my two children at no time did. I have wept again and again because Buster pushes me to places I at no time have been in my life. God loves me, and I have to remind myself of that all the time, remember that His Word is full of people that messed up.

> **Then David said to Nathan, "I have sinned against the Lord." Nathan replied, "The Lord has taken away your sin. You are not going to die. But because by doing this you have shown utter contempt for the Lord, the son born to you will die." After Nathan had gone home, the Lord struck the child that Uriah's wife had borne to David, and he became ill. David pleaded with God for the child. He fasted and spent the nights lying in sackcloth on the ground. The elders of his household stood beside him to get him up from the ground, but he refused, and he would**

not eat any food with them. On the seventh day the child died. David's attendants were afraid to tell him that the child was dead, for they thought, "While the child was still living, he wouldn't listen to us when we spoke to him. How can we now tell him the child is dead? He may do something desperate." David noticed that his attendants were whispering among themselves, and he realized the child was dead. "Is the child dead?" he asked. "Yes," they replied, "he is dead." Then David got up from the ground. After he had washed, put on lotions and changed his clothes, he went into the house of the Lord and worshiped. Then he went to his own house, and at his request they served him food, and he ate. His attendants asked him, "Why are you acting this way? While the child was alive, you fasted and wept, but now that the child is dead, you get up and eat!" He answered, "While the child was still alive, I fasted and wept. I thought, 'Who knows? The Lord may be gracious to me and let the child live.' But now that he is dead, why should I go on fasting? Can I bring him back again? I will go to him, but he will not return to me."

2 Samuel 12:13-23

David had done horrible things, and God took his child from him. Even the people around him were afraid to tell him the child was dead. In the end he recognized "my child will not come back to me, but I will go to him." Buster cannot seem to comprehend that God is in complete control over all things and can do whatever is necessary.

Buster has stolen my credit cards and debit card and taken money from me. His son is aware of it. Before school some mornings the battle is so bad Buster will stop us from leaving in the car. His little boy will tell me to hurry and lock the doors so daddy can't get in. We pray each morning before he goes into school. He prays the sweetest prayers for his mom and his dad. I have prayed some of the same prayers for years. I remind myself God is faithful please don't give up!

God is incredible. After thirty years of prayer, God has heard my cries and now my husband is with me in church every week. This is what prayer is all about. Never giving up, faithfully asking God to hear your request and knowing that what you are asking would be His Will. I go to an amazing church. The pastor and the whole staff are filled with the Holy Spirit. I went for several years by myself, and Buster would go occasionally. At one point, he even made a profession of faith. He told me recently he had to take something to keep him from being so nervous the day he was baptized. It just sickened me. When my husband came and heard the instruction of a God filled pastor his heart has become so burdened. He felt like he should have done things differently. Who in this entire world, would not go back and change things? Who doesn't think about what might have been? There is nothing to be gained by that. He told our oldest son, he was putting his foot down, and he was coming to church. Bruiser respects his father. There are things in the past he regrets, and if he could he too would change them. But he is moving forward; he now attends church with us. One Sunday both boys were at church and my husband was overcome with emotion; he looked and realized both his children were standing next to him. He began to cry. Publicly! Men rarely do this. He tells everyone after you have a grandchild this happens to you. (This is new for him) The Holy Spirit is powerful and cannot be explained!

> The joy of the Lord is your strength"
>
> Nehemiah 8:10

I have little happiness but my joy comes from the Lord. I pray a lot to find happiness again.

8

Where is the one who has been born king of the Jews? We saw his star when it rose and have come to worship him."

Matthew 2:1

My grandson has made a list of gifts he wants for Christmas. He and I went to Wal-Mart, and he sat on the floor with a pencil and looked at each item and copied down the name of what he wanted. He is a precious child. He loves for me to tell him stories before he goes to sleep each night, and these must be exceptional stories, nothing average for him. He will stop me right in the middle and tell me if it is boring, and I must start over if I have an inferior night. He goes to church with us but his dad is hit or miss, (more miss than going) so my grandson goes through times of being too tired to go. My niece has started attending church. So my grandson and great-nephew (they are two years apart) are buddies. My grandson has been talking about being baptized for a long time, but he is scared to have his head underwater. We talk about this over and over. My great-nephew is asking me several questions about being baptized. I finally told them both, when you think you can walk down and talk to the Pastor yourselves, then you will know you are big enough to ask Jesus to be the boss of your life and be baptized.

That was settled about two weeks later. During the invitation one Sunday I was in my own little world, singing, not paying much attention to anyone around me. My niece takes me by the arm, and I realize she is crying and she asks me to go down front with her. She asked Jesus into her heart, and she is happier than I have seen her in a long time. (Her Mom is my husband's sister who died of brain cancer) When the boys came out from children's church they were so excited...my great-nephew's first question "did mama walk down there all by herself?" Oh no! I have told those boys they need to do that and now look what has happened, the adult's mess things up! That is precisely how we set examples. We tell children to do something, and we do exactly the opposite. She was baptized several weeks later. As soon as she got through, (she had asked me to stand with her during her baptism) the youth pastor had said he would need to trade places with the senior pastor because a child would be baptized. I knew we needed to get out of the way and my niece is a slow mover, so I was trying to get her to go.

When I came around the corner, standing there in a little white robe was the most beautiful little boy I have ever seen. My grandson! I leaned down and asked him, "Are you sure?" He said he could do this, and he was ready! The biggest smile I have ever seen. His daddy was sobbing! (Thank God he was there that day) I ran to get my husband; he was running toward me with tears streaming down his face. God hears your prayers, please never doubt he hears them. Remember, not so long ago, I was going to church all by myself. I am not alone anymore!!

T D Jakes' said during his sermon one day that the baby Jesus never would have been found had the star not been in the sky, and you can't see the star unless it's night. Night, alone in the darkness; you can't see what is out there. The 5th graders in Sunday school, talked about the distance and time it took to travel. No use of maps and GPS, but until right this moment it never occurred to me that the traveling would have been at night to see the star as a guide. In the darkness, you depend only on God. You must put one foot in front of the other and trust He will be the guide. It's not like during the day when you can scan the distance and see what lies ahead. We all want to see the future and know that we can control something... the truth is, God is in control.

What guide am I using for my life? I need to make sure every day it is the Word of God. I have not really gotten into just how ugly things have been in my home. Some time ago... Two times I tried to kill myself. It was unbearable to keep living. I am sure you think that you would never do that. I have said the same thing. However, when your son starts from the moment, your eyes open and constantly begs for money all day you worry how you are going to live; you worry over the welfare of your grandchild until you finally reach a place you just can't go on. At that time, I felt wretched and desolate. I knew what heaven would be like and compared to what I was enduring every day and where I would spend eternity, there just wasn't any reason to stay. I begged God to help me and as always he heard me. I am writing this in obedience. This is embarrassing. Not everyone knows this, about my family or me.

Months ago, a friend I worked with lost his son. When I talked with him, I found out his son was also an addict. I had no idea. He has really had a hard time losing his son, as any father would. I was told his wife made this comment...she doesn't have to worry for her son; he is not an addict anymore. I know all about that worry. His father had done the best he could do for his children; they went to private schools, and he made sure they got what they needed. My children went to public schools and did with far less, but the path was the same. Why?

> *"For my thoughts are not your thoughts, neither are your ways my ways," declares the Lord. "As the heavens are higher than the earth, so are my ways higher than your ways and my thoughts than your thoughts.*
>
> *Isaiah 55:8-9*

God's ways are confusing. I can rejoice in so many things this year. My husband, and my oldest son are at church. My grandson has just been baptized, and you won't believe this! My great-nephew is ready and will be baptized at the service next week. My niece has been baptized and is living for the Lord. Committed to be the parent she should. I am joyful. Buster is still asking for money every day. God is in control. I trust Him.

9

For the love of money is a root of all kinds of evil.
Some people, eager for money, have wandered from
the faith and pierced themselves with many griefs.

1 Tim 6:10

Yours, Lord, is the greatness and the power and
the glory and the majesty and the splendor for
everything in heaven and earth is yours.

1 Chronicles 29:11

God owns it all. The problem, this generation believes if their parents own it, they have a right to it. I worked for the bank years when I had to leave because of my health, prior to that I worked at the grocery store for a few years. So when I tell you, I lost everything, I mean my retirement. We now live week to week. I still have money that I cannot touch until I am sixty-three. This will be the same time I will lose my long-term disability. God will still provide.

God gave me something I never deserved. I should have looked at it as the precious gift it was, and then it would not have been so easy for me to freely allow my son to blind my eyes. I now must face all I worked for is gone. Being angry and bitter will not earn it back. I can't return to the bank and start over. I can't get another job and just earn it back. I now have a fixed income, and the debts make it hard to live each month. Should my son be paying the debts? He should! He should desire to do so. Even so, the money he has taken he can never repay in this lifetime. He has no college education, by choice. As a parent, you hope to help your child, but when they refuse help and don't want help it is devastating to watch them destroy themselves and others they love. At this point, it has been years since he has had a job.

Your suggestion, I'm sure is to put him on the streets...is it really? Look at your child today and decide to actually put them in the street. Now remember he has a little boy who adores him. Not so easy is it? It is like being tormented every day. God knows what is going on. Think back over the situations in the Bible. Mary was chosen to have Jesus and the struggle she faced was so hard. She watched her son get beaten and die. God never promises us easy choices. He promises to never leave you or forsake you. Jesus never did one thing wrong; that's definitely not the case here.

We sometimes bring on our own trouble. Granted things may be unjust, but God trusts us with problems. He expects us to lean on Him and then, and only then can our Faith grow. If everything is given and nothing ever goes wrong, you would never need to depend on God. God gave His son, and we make promises to him all the time. Years ago, people made financial agreements without signing contracts, a handshake and their word was enough. A man's word meant something. But people today have no idea that God still feels the same way. God does not change as the times; He expects us to be serious with the words we speak.

In the following story, you will find just how serious a vow is to God. Words cause damage to you and sometimes to the people we love.

Jephthah the Gileadite was a mighty warrior. His father was Gilead; his mother was a prostitute. Gilead's wife also bore him sons, and when they were grown up, they drove Jephthah away. "You are not going to get any inheritance in our family," they said, "because you are the son of another woman." So Jephthah fled from his brothers and settled in the land of Tob, where a gang of scoundrels gathered around him and followed him. Sometime later, when the Ammonites were fighting against Israel, the elders of Gilead went to get Jephthah from the land of Tob. "Come," they said, "be our commander, so we can fight the Ammonites." Jephthah said to them, "Didn't you hate me and drive me from my father's house? Why do you come to me now, when you're in trouble?" The elders of Gilead said to him, "Nevertheless, we are turning to you now; come with us to fight the Ammonites, and you will be head over all of us who live in Gilead." Jephthah answered, "Suppose you take me back to fight the Ammonites and the Lord gives them to me—will I really be your head?" The elders of Gilead replied, "The Lord is our witness; we will certainly do as you say." So Jephthah went with the elders of Gilead, and the people made him head and commander over them. And he repeated all his words before the

Lord in Mizpah. Then Jephthah sent messengers to the Ammonite king with the question: "What do you have against me that you have attacked my country?" The king of the Ammonites answered Jephthah's messengers, "When Israel came up out of Egypt, they took away my land from the Arnon to the Jabbok, all the way to the Jordan. Now give it back peaceably." Jephthah sent back messengers to the Ammonite king, saying: "This is what Jephthah says: Israel did not take the land of Moab or the land of the Ammonites. But when they came up out of Egypt, Israel went through the wilderness to the Red Sea and on to Kadesh. Then Israel sent messengers to the king of Edom, saying, 'Give us permission to go through your country,' but the king of Edom would not listen. They sent also to the king of Moab, and he refused. So Israel stayed at Kadesh. "Next they traveled through the wilderness, skirted the lands of Edom and Moab, passed along the eastern side of the country of Moab, and camped on the other side of the Arnon. They did not enter the territory of Moab, for the Arnon was its border. "Then Israel sent messengers to Sihon king of the Amorites, who ruled in Heshbon, and said to him, 'Let us pass through your country to our own place.' Sihon, however, did not trust Israel to pass through his territory. He mustered all his troops and encamped at Jahaz and fought with Israel. "Then the Lord, the God of Israel, gave Sihon and his whole army into Israel's hands, and they defeated them. Israel took over all the land of the Amorites who lived in that country, capturing all of it from the Arnon to the Jabbok and from the desert to the Jordan. "Now since the Lord, the God of Israel, has driven the Amorites out before his people Israel, what right have you to take it over?

Will you not take what your god Chemosh gives you? Likewise, whatever the Lord our God has given us, we will possess. Are you any better than Balak son of Zippor, king of Moab? Did he ever quarrel with Israel or fight with them? For three hundred years Israel occupied Heshbon, Aroer, the surrounding settlements and all the towns along the Arnon. Why didn't you retake them? I have not wronged you, but you are doing me wrong by waging war against me. Let the Lord, the Judge, decide the dispute this day between the Israelites and the Ammonites." The king of Ammon, however, paid no attention to the message Jephthah sent him. Then the Spirit of the Lord came on Jephthah. He crossed Gilead and Manasseh, passed through Mizpah of Gilead, and from there he advanced against the Ammonites. And Jephthah made a vow to the Lord: "If you give the Ammonites into my hands, whatever comes out of the door of my house to meet me when I return in triumph from the Ammonites will be the Lord's, and I will sacrifice it as a burnt offering." Then Jephthah went over to fight the Ammonites, and the Lord gave them into his hands. He devastated twenty towns from Aroer to the vicinity of Minnith, as far as Abel Keramim.

Thus Israel subdued Ammon. When Jephthah returned to his home in Mizpah, who should come out to meet him but his daughter, dancing to the sound of timbrels! She was an only child. Except for her he had neither son nor daughter. When he saw her, he tore his clothes and cried, "Oh no, my daughter! You have brought me down and I am devastated. I have made a vow to the Lord that I cannot break." "My father," she replied, "you have given your word to the Lord. Do to me just as you promised, now that the Lord has avenged you of your enemies, the Ammonites. But grant me this one request," she said. "Give me two months to roam the hills and weep with my friends, because I will never marry." "You may go," he said. And he let her go for two months. She and her friends went into the hills and wept because she would never marry. After the two months, she returned to her father, and he did to her as he had vowed. And she was a virgin. From this comes the Israelite tradition that each year the young women of Israel go out for four days to commemorate the daughter of Jephthah the Gileadite.

Judges 11:1-40

Jephthah made a vow and now he was bound by his word to keep it. The words of his own mouth destroyed the child he loved. Words destroy. Once they are said they cannot be taken back. They destroy years of love and joy.

This pain is unexplainable, and I hope that reading this will prevent anyone else from ever facing this kind of loss. We have lost years that cannot be replaced, family that I don't think will forever understand much less be forgiving and years of love and trust. We have no money for Christmas, and our sole focus was on our grandson, a small gift to our great-nephews and a couple of minor things to our son and his girlfriend. I made some of those gifts. I'm talking boxers and some church shirts with ties (you know the kinds of things that last a long time) nothing that would be a luxury. I love to read, and was surprised to receive a Kindle-fire from my husband. We had been hanging our towels all over the house to dry because the dryer was out of commission, and my husband was looking for the part on the Internet. I first felt so guilty about the gift, but he wanted me to have it and he was so happy when he gave it. Two days after Christmas Buster stole my gift and sold it. He denied it, got mad WE would even think to accuse him. This is the life I face daily; an addict must have money every day. If you leave your home, things may disappear. He has sold or pawned over half of his dad's good tools. He sold a ring my husband received when his uncle died it can never be replaced. The list goes on and on. Even Buster's son has asked repeatedly how his dad can get in and out of a room without making any noise. We lock our bedroom and have bolted a safe in the closet to protect medications we have to take. We placed the credit cards (that now have balances) in the safe because nothing is safe with him in our home.

We truly fear leaving our home because you do not know what will be gone when we return. It is like living in a prison. I fear that in my future, I will have to have my son arrested, and if I do what will my grandson think of me? God tells us to love and to forgive. Jesus forgives us. How much more of this can I take? Buster just keeps taking more and more and expects that we understand and forgive. Do I do that to God? Do I ask anew and expect more and get angry when He doesn't answer me the way I want Him to? Is this difficult situation showing me that my prayers are stingy, and I do not think of what God would ask of me? I am the reason Jesus had to die; I keep making mistakes over and over. This is why I keep myself in God's Word and why I ask for forgiveness all the time. I know I am not what I need to be, and that is why I struggle with having my son arrested. The example I set will have repercussions for life, is it worth that?

10

"Holy, holy, holy is the Lord Almighty; The whole earth is full of his glory."

Isaiah 6:3

Good judgment wins favor, but the way of the unfaithful leads to their destruction

Proverbs 13:15

The real problem with most young parents today is they have no faith, so they have no place to start. With faith, you can study and listen to God speak to you and direct your life, but these people are headed for destruction and taking these little children with them. Good judgment comes with age but at the detriment of the children, which is not a luxury we can afford any longer. Taking pills and drinking to calm down to get through the day or through the night is not how you take care of your responsibilities. God's Word has an answer for all problems. If all the children of these addicts grow up to be addicts, our world will become more unstable and unsafe.

I have studied God's Word through Beth Moore Studies and at our church. I facilitate those studies (you don't really teach) we talk through a lot of things. I have always been involved teaching in church so that keeps you in God's Word. God reveals to us through his Word and speaks if we just ask. This is the where he takes me many times.

> *In the year that King Uzziah died, I saw the Lord, high and exalted, seated on a throne; and the train of his robe filled the temple. Above him were seraphim, each with six wings: With two wings they covered their faces, with two they covered their feet, and with two they were flying. And they were calling to one another: "Holy, holy, holy is the Lord Almighty; the whole earth is full of his glory." At the sound of their voices the doorposts and thresholds shook and the temple was filled with smoke. "Woe to me!" I cried. "I am ruined! For I am a man of unclean lips, and I live among a people of unclean lips, and my eyes have seen the King, the Lord Almighty." Then one of the seraphim flew to me with a live coal in his hand, which he had taken with tongs from the altar. With it he touched my mouth and said, "See, this has touched your lips; your guilt is taken away and your sin atoned for." Then I heard the voice of the Lord saying, "Whom shall I send? And who will go for us?" And I said, "Here am I. Send me!" He said, "Go and tell this people: "Be ever hearing, but never understanding; be ever seeing, but never perceiving.' Make the heart of this people calloused; make their ears dull and close their eyes. Otherwise they might see with their eyes, hear with*

> **their ears, understand with their hearts, and turn**
> **and be healed." Then I said, "For how long, Lord?"**
> **Isaiah 6:1-11**

When I read these scriptures, (even today) I weep. I am a woman of unclean lips and I live in a home of unclean lips. But I have seen The King, The Lord!! It makes me come before Him on my face and beg to be forgiven, for all the things that have passed through these lips that have caused pain and hurt. These lips he created to share the gospel and tell the story of a birth, death and resurrection and how no one must die and be separated from JESUS, the one that did die! Isaiah recognized the same thing, and the Angels came and cauterized his lips. Mine must be cauterized and many times just sewn together to keep them completely shut.

Most of the people that are addicts are just like the people God is describing. I see my son in these verses. He hears but acts as though he does not understand, he sees but cannot perceive. His heart has become calloused; his ears are dull, and he has closed his eyes to God. I pray for healing. I beg God to know, How Long?

I explained to you earlier that God had answered my prayers, not in my timing but in His timing. He is a mighty God, and I have a personal relationship with Him. He hears my voice. I have given you many examples of his communication with me through His Word. He would speak in a service, and it would overwhelm me, because He would answer me with Words. When you recognize God operates this way look back at those scriptures. The angels do His work, and if you notice they cover their eyes with two wings, feet with two wings and fly with the other two, the wind and the shout of their voices caused the temple to shake. God has no relationship with them. HE does with

US. YOU and I! My child is trading all that I have described for pills and lies. It is so sad. Time on this earth is so short.

> ***A thousand years in your sight are like a day that***
> ***has just gone by, or like a watch in the night.***
> ***Psalm 90: 4***

We have been told that Jesus has been gone from this earth two thousand years; if that is the case, he left here two days ago as far as he is concerned. He is not slow in coming. He is giving an opportunity for ALL to come to know Him and none to die and be separated from Him and go to Hell. If you know more about the timing, and he has been gone longer, his timing still has not changed, He has only been gone from this earth a few days, and it is the people here he has left to do the work. Look around you...who is telling the kids about Jesus? You can't talk about it at school. Most parents know nothing. Grandparents throw their hands up and say what is the use. Jesus will ask us what we did.

11

"You have heard that it was said, 'Love your neighbor and hate your enemy.' But I tell you love your enemies and pray for those who persecute you, that you may be children of your Father in heaven. He causes his sun to rise on the evil and the good, and sends rain on the righteous and the unrighteous.

Matthew 5:43-45

Loving everyone is hard, and pleasing everyone is impossible. My family does not understand the circumstances we live in. We don't go out to eat or visit, explaining is the hardest part. This book is the closest I will ever come to explain something that cannot be understood. Buster's need for these pills is so bad he has asked everyone he knows for money. If he does not get them every day, he is sick. However, he still denies that he needs help. We have threatened Buster not to go to any family member and ask for money. Nothing works.

It reminds me of the story in the Bible of an evil man. But he met up with the wrong WOMAN. This man was trying to destroy the whole nation of Jews, and God would never allow that. The book of Esther is awesome. God is never one time mentioned, but the whole nation of Jews is talked about, and God is implied throughout the book. This has happened repeatedly in history God will always protect His people. This is the story when Haman which thought he was so clever, got found out.

> *So the king and Haman went to Queen Esther's banquet, and as they were drinking wine on the second day, the king again asked, "Queen Esther, what is your petition? It will be given you. What is your request? Even up to half the kingdom, it will be granted." Then Queen Esther answered, "If I have found favor with you, Your Majesty, and if it pleases you, grant me my life—this is my petition. And spare my people—this is my request. For I and my people have been sold to be destroyed, killed and annihilated. If we had merely been sold as male and female slaves, I would have kept quiet, because no such distress would justify disturbing the king." King Xerxes asked Queen Esther, "Who is he? Where is he—the man who has dared to do such a thing?" Esther said, "An adversary and enemy! This vile Haman!" Then Haman was terrified before the king and queen. The king got up in a rage, left his wine and went out into the palace garden. But Haman, realizing that the king had already decided his fate, stayed behind to beg Queen Esther for his life.*
>
> *Esther 7:1-7*

Esther was a teenage girl. She could have gotten anything she wanted...freedom, money (he offered her up to half of his kingdom), but she was wise. She asked that her people be spared. She even told him if all that would happen was for them to be sold into slavery, she would have said nothing...but Haman was going to kill a whole group of people because they were Jewish. Read the story, Haman decided his own fate. That happens to addicts, they choose for themselves what will transpire in their lives. They lose their teeth, their families, and ability to get jobs. Their bodies will eventually be unable to tolerate the pills or whatever choice of drug they use. Liver, kidney and heart can only tolerate so much. Although, the largest waste is they miss what path God had for them to travel. They had a choice. There were two paths, a right way and a wrong way. There still is a choice, but have they waited so long that a lot of the bridges have been burned, and they can no longer cross them? God is at the end of every road. Everyone meets Him at the end.

> *It is written: "'As surely as I live,' says the Lord, 'every knee will bow before me; every tongue will acknowledge God.'" So then, each of us will give an account of ourselves to God.*
>
> *Romans 14: 11-12*

> *And I saw the dead, great and small, standing before the throne, and books were opened. Then another book was opened, which is the book of life. And the dead were judged by what was written in the books, according to what they had done.*
>
> *Revelation 20:12*

If we ask for forgiveness God forgives us, but how can an unsaved person talk to God at all? God gives us all the chance to turn our life over to him and allow Him to lead us, but if we say He is Lord of our life, and we continue to live as we constantly have how you can say that? The Savior of the World is our Lord, and we continue to behave as we always have. What an awful embarrassment for our Lord.... how would you feel if your child was drunk and falling down announcing to the world you were the parent? Humiliated? OR It would be like saying you're in love with someone and being unfaithful to him or her every day of every week and expecting them to understand and not be upset about it. Would you tolerate that?

Who would stay in a relationship with you this way? Remember God allowed his only Son, to die a horrible death, and you are supposed to have accepted him as Lord of All, yet you never think of His Word, His Will, and His Way...what kind of relationship is that? The things you think are so important. What does He think about them? His Word tells us what to think about.

> *Finally, brothers and sisters, whatever is true, whatever is noble, whatever is right, whatever is pure, whatever is lovely, whatever is admirable—if anything is excellent or praiseworthy—think about such things.*
>
> *Philippians 4:8*

The problem today and not just addicts, most people do not think about any of these things people in general consider themselves first. What do I need today? When I was a teenager, I went to a retreat and was taught to have a quiet time with God every day. A time of prayer and just a Bible verse or two but it was how you started every day.

In the day, we live; everyone has a devotional for sale. Something you can use as a guide if you find it difficult to do alone. If everyone started their day this way, you would find that things in your life would make a drastic change. You may not see improvement at first, especially if you do not like instruction and direction. Obedience will result in blessings. Remember I had to pray for years for some of my answers, but not all the things I prayed for took that long.

I can think of one instance where God answered one of the children's prayers in Sunday school. At the end of every class, we discuss prayer requests. For two months, this fifth grader was concerned with the salvation of her grandfather. She walked through the sanctuary one Sunday afternoon with me, and we were praying at each pew about the service. She stopped and fell at a spot and cried for her grandfather; I prayed with her. Not long after, he began attending. He is now a deacon, and he sits right in the spot she had her head laying on the pew weeping for him. (I told him about it sometime later) This is the Greatness of our God! She got to see God answer her prayers. She is faithful and as a young woman, she is not afraid to sing at church. Her entire family now attends our church. Recently, the whole community prayed for her aunt who went through a 1-year battle with breast cancer, but she has been healed. God answers prayers! This is how prayer, faith and church work together! It is important for everyone to surround themselves with people of faith when things are hard. Addiction can be so many things, but God can heal you if you want to be well.

I have told you about my battle-scarred home life.... is yours like mine? You may not have a problem with an addict who has led to financial ruin. Maybe yours is anger you cannot control and because of it; you are lonely and cannot have normal relationships with other people. Could you have a gambling problem? You play bingo with every extra dime you have, what started as fun has turned into an obsession you cannot control? Maybe it's cards, dice or drinking? It could be a spending habit or a hoarding issue. You feel the need to surround yourself with things so you feel treasured since no one ever made you feel that way. Could you have a food addiction; you eat to soothe yourself even when you're not hungry? These are the same cravings the addict has, but you crave something that the police will not put you in jail for. The body will end up in the same condition as an addict, the heart, the liver they are working too hard, but no one likes to think about this.

All these are addictions, whether you want to call them that or not. They cause you and those who love you pain. Sometimes they can cost your loved ones everything. Some of your loved ones have a hard time understanding this. I will admit this can be how I react immediately.

My oldest son, Bruiser, has low tolerance for this type of behavior. He loves to play golf. He chose this sport, one because he loved it and second because this sport was totally his responsibility. He cannot blame someone else for the winning or losing. If he makes a mistake, it is his own. That is how he feels about addicts. If they want to stop something, they should make up their minds and stop. Period, just stop. He has a friend, who was an alcoholic, but he overcame his addiction, and now he works where they serve alcohol and he does not drink. He is not tempted; he just made a choice not to be that person anymore.

I suppose some people have that ability; I have no kind of statistics, but I would think that would be hard and few people would fall within that category. I think that is why they have all the programs for people to go to.......... provide them support.

What I have the least tolerance for, is lies and lack of admission to the real problem.

> ***For all have sinned and fall short of the glory of God***
> ***Romans 3:23***

The Bible says we all are the same as far as making mistakes. So saying out loud that I have messed up is not that big an issue. However, the addicts I have been around will lie when the truth would have been more appropriate. Why? They steal, and then lie about it, and you know they have done it. The same is true for God. Why do we do the same things with God? He sees right through our lies, yet we continue to do the same thing over and over. God knows that we were born a sinner, the scripture above tells us so. He provided a way for us to be free from this life.

> ***For God so loved the world that he gave his one and only Son, that whoever believes in him shall not perish but have eternal life.***
> ***John 3:16***

We make a choice. The addicts make a choice. Are you an addict?

12

He not only considered it trivial to commit the sins of Jeroboam son of Nebat, but he also married Jezebel daughter of Ethbaal king of the Sidonians, and began to serve Baal and worship him.

1 Kings 16:31

Have you ever done something in your life that, at the time seemed trivial? Ahab married Jezebel and he did not think too much about it. Really, is it anyone's business that we marry? She went to a different church does that matter either? So what if God's Word says her husband is to be the head of the household and the leader in the home? You all know what disobedience is like.

It is better to live in a corner of the housetop than in a house shared with a quarrelsome wife.

Proverbs 21:9

Even God's Word will back you up if you get a bad woman. But be warned do not twist God's word to use to your advantage; God would never be pleased by that. Even so, what Ahab did was against everything God required. She was not a woman within his faith, and she served another god; she was a strong-willed woman who had a way of making her way known and getting what she demanded. He was headed for destruction.

There was a great man of God named Elijah; he was a prophet, and he knew about the people worshiping Baal. He knew God was not happy and would deal with the people regarding their disobedience.

So Obadiah went to meet Ahab and told him, and Ahab went to meet Elijah. When he saw Elijah, he said to him, "Is that you, you troubler of Israel?" "I have not made trouble for Israel," Elijah replied. "But you and your father's family have. You have abandoned the Lord's commands and have followed the Baals. Now summon the people from all over Israel to meet me on Mount Carmel. And bring the four hundred and fifty prophets of Baal and the four hundred prophets of Asherah, who eat at Jezebel's table." So Ahab sent word throughout all Israel and assembled the prophets on Mount Carmel. Elijah went before the people and said, "How long will you waver between two opinions? If The Lord is God, follow him; but if Baal is God, follow him." But the people said nothing. Then Elijah said to them, "I am the only one of the Lord's prophets left, but Baal has four hundred and fifty prophets. Get two bulls for us. Let Baal's prophets choose one for themselves, and let them cut it into pieces and put it on the wood but not set fire to it. I will prepare the other bull and put it on the wood but not set fire to it. Then you call on the name of your god, and I will call on the name of the Lord. The god who answers by fire—he is God." Then all the people said, "What you say is good." Elijah said to the prophets of Baal, "Choose one of the bulls and prepare it first, since there are so many of you. Call on the name of your god, but do not light the fire." So they took the bull given them and prepared it. Then they called on the name of Baal from morning till noon. "Baal, answer us!" they shouted. But there was no response; no one answered. And they danced around the altar they had made. At noon Elijah began to taunt them. "Shout louder!" he said. "Surely he is a god! Perhaps he is deep in thought, or busy, or traveling. Maybe he is sleeping and must be awakened." So they shouted louder and slashed themselves with swords and spears, as was their custom, until their blood flowed. Midday passed, and they continued their frantic prophesying until the time for the evening sacrifice. But there was no response, no one answered, and no one paid attention. Then Elijah said to all the people, "Come here to me." They came to him, and he repaired the altar of the Lord, which had been torn down. Elijah took twelve stones, one for each of the tribes descended from Jacob, to whom the word of the Lord had come, saying, "Your name shall be Israel." With the stones he built an altar in the name of the Lord, and he dug a trench around it large enough to hold two seahs of seed. He arranged the wood, cut the bull into pieces and laid it on the wood. Then he said to them, "Fill four large jars with water and pour it on the offering and on the wood." "Do it again," he said, and they did it again. Then the fire of the Lord fell and burned up the sacrifice, the wood, the stones and the soil, and also licked up the water in the trench. When all the people saw this, they fell prostrate and cried, "The Lord—he is God! The Lord—he is God!" Then Elijah commanded them, "Seize the prophets of Baal. Don't let anyone get away!" They seized them, and Elijah had them brought down to the Kishon Valley and slaughtered there. And Elijah said to Ahab, "Go, eat and drink, for there is the sound of a heavy rain." So Ahab went off to eat and drink, but Elijah climbed to the top of Carmel, bent down to the ground and put his face between his knees. "Go and look toward the sea," he told his servant. And he went up and looked. "There is nothing there," he said. Seven times Elijah said, "Go back." The seventh time the servant reported, "A cloud as small as a man's hand is rising from the sea." So Elijah said, "Go and tell Ahab, 'Hitch up your chariot and go down before the rain stops you.'" Meanwhile, the sky grew black with clouds, the wind rose, a heavy rain started falling and Ahab rode off to Jezreel. The power of the Lord came on Elijah and, tucking his cloak into his belt, he ran ahead of Ahab all the way to Jezreel.

1Kings 18: 16-46

Elijah knew God was the only God and the people had to be shown. We live the same way.... we want miracles, and we want to see the same things these people do and when it doesn't happen like it did in the Bible people today say.... Where is God? On the other hand, people today say there is no God. Nevertheless, you will find these men were weak too. There were 450 prophets for Baal and 400 prophets for Asherah, and these men had been eating from the table of Jezebel. Elijah serves one God, the TRUE GOD. God destroyed by fire what they sacrificed with water. That is how God will work in your situation it will not always be logical to you. God is the one that receives the glory. As long as you are trying to do anything by yourself, He will allow you to keep going until you realize how much you need Him. Ahab went home to tell Jezebel everything that happened, and she was not happy about it at all. Remember those men were at her table, she was the one controlling them and now Elijah has gotten into her business. She is going to take care of him. Get in God's Word and find out what happened. I have tried to give you strong people with real problems that overcame them, but God trusted them enough to deal with a problem and to see it through to the end. If you never have a problem, you won't need God for anything. People today have the same spirit as Jezebel. She manipulated; she controlled. When she was after Elijah, she was mean at the point of being out to destroy him. Although she was destroying Ahab too, by a different means, sweet, charming, loving, but she was still the same person. She was out to destroy all who were in her way.

You know these people; you may be this person and not realize that you are. You disapprove everything going on in the church that does not include you and more important it should have been your idea. You interject yourselves in the middle of all things. These people will lie and believe their own lies. Usually, this person is a woman. One you have loved and trusted. Most feel a power when they have accomplished the task they set out to complete. Whether it is to destroy another person, stop the growth of a group of people or an individual, tell a part truth that mars the peace and happiness of a group or an individual for a long time. You always question why? Why me? What did I do to cause those feelings in that person? Real repentance is the only answer for them. Forgiveness to this person could mean an open door to opportunity to begin a new cycle of the Jezebel Spirit all over again.

Many people have the ability to manipulate, cheat, lie and steal and feel absolutely no remorse for it. Men and Women. This is not just a problem throughout the world it is in the church. You want so badly to trust everyone, but that is impossible. Remember, Judas walked right in the midst of the apostles, and he had no problem when selling Jesus for the thirty pieces of silver. Jesus knew that the betrayer was there. Did he know all the time?

> **But Jesus said to him, "Judas, would you betray the Son of Man with a kiss?"**
>
> *Luke 22:48*

Never in a million years, would I have believed that a child I loved so deeply and dedicated to God would betray me the way this one has. My heart breaks for my grandchild. I fear for him because his future is so unsure. He needs role models who are Christians. My oldest son has no children. I think that my grandson is not sure he can love his uncle because it might hurt his dad. Children comprehend considerably more than you and I perpetually give them credit. As a child, his prayers are substantially more to the point than most adults ever say. His heart is pure. He wants God to do what will make his Dad get healthy and love "him" (his son). He even told God one day, that wasn't a lot for Him (God) to do.

My grandson's desire is for his Dad's health and love. We fail to be honest with God; we tend to petition God for possessions, moving swiftly to things of fascination and greed. Nevertheless, children speak from the depths of the heart and tend to show concern for others, failing often to mention any desire they might have. God loves us too much to allow us to have those things. And as I explained to my grandson, he would be healthy and healed when he desires it as much as we want it for him. God desires that for all of us, have you ever thought about that? Are you asking God to do things you know for sure are His Will? Begging for things you know He would at no time allow you to do because it is not in keeping with His Word. God would never desire parents of a child to be addicts... God's Will is for you to be healed today. Growing up I was taught if you sleep with dogs you get fleas. I'm not saying all addicts are dogs but the activities they participate in lead to other poor decisions and behaviors that are not acceptable for children to be exposed to. Fleas if dealt with immediately are easy to stop. You must destroy the source. I don't mean an animal carrying the fleas must be destroyed, but you must find the source of the fleas. If not, as long as you go back near the source, fleas will continue to become more and more infested, first with itching, then with sores, and finally you will have to get some medical attention. Until one day, you will become a source just like in the beginning someone else was. Addictions are no different. If you surround yourselves with people that have the same desires, you will never make a change. Eventually, it will drive you crazy. There was a man in the Bible that God allowed to become king because the people wanted a king. There is only one True KING OF KINGS.

Kish had a son named Saul, as handsome a young
man as could be found anywhere in Israel, and he

was a head taller than anyone else. Now the day before Saul came, the Lord had revealed this to Samuel: "About this time tomorrow I will send you a man from the land of Benjamin. Anoint him ruler over my people Israel; he will deliver them from the hand of the Philistines. I have looked on my people, for their cry has reached me When Samuel caught sight of Saul, the Lord said to him, "This is the man I spoke to you about; he will govern my people."

1 Samuel 9:2, 15-17

In the scriptures above you will see God chose Saul and Saul succeeded in many wars. God gave him Samuel the prophet to speak to him directly from God. Remember there was no Bible to consult. There were times Saul rejoiced in the Lord with the people. Samuel spoke to the king and the people and warned them.

If you will fear the Lord and serve him and obey his voice and not rebel against the commandment of the Lord, and if both you and the king who reigns over you will follow the Lord your God, it will be well. But if you will not obey the voice of the Lord, but rebel against the commandment of the Lord, then the hand of the Lord will be against you and your king.

1 Samuel 12:14-15

Saul became his own enemy. He was only thirty when he became king. He reigned forty-two years. I am hoping if you have taken time to read this, and you are young you won't be foolish enough to make the mistakes that Saul did or I did. Saul's name means "asked" in Hebrew. He thought he was special. You know the type, tall, dark and handsome. That is the description used in the Bible. He would be what the world is full of today. Entitled. A well-to-do family, plus good looking, he had all the world would see as successful. But the real problem was he knew that he was special. You need to know there will always be someone "after you." Samuel had left him, so he no longer had God speaking to him, and he went his own way.

> *Saul said to Samuel, "I have sinned, for I have transgressed the commandment of the Lord and your words, because I feared the people and obeyed their voice*
>
> *1 Samuel 15:24*

Samuel returned to Saul and told him what God had said. Finally, Saul admits to the sins he has committed. God always knows what is going on in our life. We don't have to be a king or a prophet. Read this entire story and see all the people affected by these choices. God had a plan. God has given us the same command he gave to Saul...

> *Until the day, Samuel died, he did not go to see Saul again, though Samuel mourned for him. And the LORD regretted that he had made Saul king over Israel.*
>
> *1 Samuel 15:35*

Samuel grieved over Saul. Saul recognized that he had sinned. We all have sinned, and we will again. For the first time in this study of the first king God chose, I saw how God felt. I really don't think I had ever thought that God might have regretted anything. I looked up several translations of this verse, most said regretted, one said repented. But the issue is that the Lord did what the children of Israel asked...he gave them a king. God is our King. It amounted to the children you love wanting another Father. He loved them, took care of them, and they wanted someone else. How hurtful it was and is every day. We still reject him every choice that goes against His Will, His Word and His Plan. You choose another Father.

I would choose for my son to change today. I cannot change him, only God can. He is my son, and I love him even though he has hurt me. I am God's child, and I wonder how many times he has had to say; she is my child; I love her even though she has hurt me. What about you? I do not want to stand before His Throne and have Him say, I regret......... God cannot lie. He will not welcome you home; home is for family, are you in the family of God?

Does any of these addictions sound like your story? Do you want to have a relationship with God so that you never fear being all alone and searching for comfort in a substance or food or trying to find a person to make you feel good about yourself? Find a friend or a family member, seek a pastor to talk to today, please don't wait. God never promises us tomorrow use the time now for good and great things for Him!

> *For God says, "At just the right time, I heard you.*
> *On the day of salvation, I helped you." Indeed, the*
> *"right time" is now. Today is the day of salvation.*
> *2 Corinthians 6:2*

13

"Therefore if any man be in Christ, he is a new creature: old things are passed away behold, all things are become new."

2 Corinthians 5:17

Do you remember the person you were before Jesus was the Lord of your life? Would you be the one to reveal a person's past even though they are trying hard to move past it and forget it? In the world we live, no one allows things to be kept secret too much anymore. You Tube can send out a message that can haunt you forever. Except, have you been in some situations that unless you were there you just could not explain the events to another person? John the Baptist and Jesus were cousins. They were about six months apart in age. God had a special hand in both births. In the time period, they were born your son was always named after his father. John's father was a priest from Jerusalem. You may never have thought a lot about the priests but there is an important fact you must never overlook again.

The LORD said to Aaron, "You will have no inheritance in their land, nor will you have any

> **share among them; I am your share and your**
> **inheritance among the Israelites.**
>
> *Numbers 18:20*

God was their share! The priests had a special relationship; none of the other brothers could receive. All the others got land, but the priests had an intimate relationship with God. They went into the tabernacle and offered sacrifices, and no one else could go there. God is their portion. We sing a song today that says Jesus is our portion; it is not a matter of words that is a big thing. He is our priest. We get to be new creatures because of what He did. John the Baptist was not like his father. He told everyone about the Messiah coming. He received this confirmation when he baptized Jesus.

> **Then Jesus came from Galilee to the Jordan to be**
> **baptized by John. But John tried to deter him, saying,**
> **"I need to be baptized by you, and do you come to me?"**
> **Jesus replied, "Let it be so now; it is proper for us to do**
> **this to fulfill all righteousness." Then John consented.**
> **As soon as Jesus was baptized, he went up out of the**
> **water. At that moment heaven was opened, and he saw**
> **the Spirit of God descending like a dove and alighting**
> **on him. And a voice from heaven said, "This is my**
> **Son, whom I love; with him I am well pleased."**
>
> *Matthew 3:13-17*

John is being obedient to do what he knows God sent him to do. Our struggle is because we are not sure what God has called us to do. John was called to be different. We have trouble with this part, as long as God lets us look like everyone else and be a part of the same group as all our friends then obedience is not a problem. Save for John lived among the woods and ate bugs and honey. We are not willing to be inconvenienced.

> *After Jesus had finished instructing his twelve disciples, he went on from there to teach and preach in the towns of Galilee. When John, who was in prison, heard about the deeds of the Messiah, he sent his disciples to ask him, "Are you the one who is to come, or should we expect someone else?" Jesus replied, "Go back and report to John what you hear and see: The blind receive sight, the lame walk, those who have leprosy are cleansed, the deaf hear, the dead are raised, and the good news is proclaimed to the poor. Blessed is anyone who does not stumble on account of me."*
>
> *Matthew 11: 1-6*

Did you just read that? John, who had baptized Jesus, sends some of the people following him around to ask...Are you the one? Should we look for someone else? John who heard the heavens speak; this is my SON, in whom I AM WELL PLEASED. How can you hear that and then ask that question? John was in prison; inside there a man might think a lot of things he might not if he were walking around in the free world.

I am faced with a decision I don't want to ever have to deal with. Our life is a daily challenge; Buster asks for money every day, and we don't have it to give. Desperation sets in when you don't get what it is you want or according to him, you need. One day, it is the same scenario, before school we fight and when I come home something in my home is peculiar. A long time ago we put a dead bolt on our bedroom door. This did not stop things from disappearing so we purchased a safe we mounted in the closet. When I got home, the bedroom door was ajar. I knew that I had locked it. Buster tried to convince me I had left it open, but I was certain that I would secure that door. In the safe are medications my husband, and I must take; we have credit cards that have balances on them because of Buster, there is no money left, and he has gotten and sold all the jewelry that had any value. I waited until noon and called my husband at lunch. He asked me if I checked to see if my Kindle-fire was in the room. The instant he mentioned that I went to investigate, and it was missing. The last time he got it, he took it to a pawnshop, and we had to pay forty-eight dollars to get it back. I confronted him and as usual he knew nothing about it. I checked to see if my grandson's tablet (like my Kindle) was in his room, and it was gone too. Buster now is enraged, how could I accuse him of taking his own child's game; he would never do that? What kind of person do I think he is? This is my breaking point. I went back to my room and looked around and realize he has busted the door, you can't tell from the front but the back is crushed. I tell my husband what I am going to do. He finally gives me his approval to call the police... (Up to this point; he has been the one to stop me each time I was ready) I asked him to come home and help me, but he said he couldn't.

Buster does not believe I will make the phone call to have him arrested. He is on the phone, telling me he has a few minutes left to get our Kindles back or we won't be able to get them. I call the police department. He now picks up the phone and tells them to destroy the Kindles because I have called the police. He is so upset that I would have him arrested. He reminds me I am his mother.

All the years I worked in the bank, we would load the ATM with money and that required having the police come each day to the bank. The policeman I call is a friend; they remember when I had this child. They are sad for me and want to help. They have to make pictures of the broken door. When they take Buster's billfold, inside are two pawn slips. One for each Kindle. They had to handcuff him and take him to the station. He still keeps insisting that he has no drug problem. He won't tell them anything.

When my grandson comes home, I have to tell him what I have done. He is not mad at me; he just wants his daddy to get better and for the two of them to get a house together. He says he knew daddy was taking his game, because some men came to the door and would kill him if he didn't give them some money. My grandson said he wanted his daddy more than his game. It breaks my heart.

The moment Buster is in jail he called and asked us to get him out. I told him there is not a chance. Every day he calls begging to come home. Finally, he wants me to send him some Bible Studies. He is reading his Bible but would like me to help him with his study. My grandson writes a letter, with lots of exclamation points behind, I Love You. He wrote the whole thing himself. It is beautiful. We sent him two pictures. He finished the Bible Studies quickly. Two other men read them again and again and have asked if I could send them more letters with the studies included. One of the men is older and will be there for four years, Buster said he read the letter at least twenty times.

Do we realize we could share in a letter; information that might mean salvation to a man or woman that has limited resources and understanding? We go to church and classes every week and sit back and get fat on God's Word. It's like being a glutton; we hoard it and never share with anyone. That is wrong. I don't mean you share details about your life, but writing an in depth Bible Study is not too hard if you read God's Word. You share scripture and give them places to look up and work for themselves. It will bless you and them.

When you plan your life, and you desire children, it would never enter your mind, as the mother of this child, that protects and helps to dress him, feeds him, holds this little boy when he would cry, I have had him arrested. I cannot put into words the pain I feel. There are no words to convey my feelings, devastated, crushed, hurt, none of these come close to describe how I feel. God knows; His Son was arrested too. I keep talking to Him, and he reassures me; things will get better. I will be so glad to see that day come.

14

O God, listen to my cry! Hear my prayer! From the ends of the earth, I cry to you for help when my heart is overwhelmed. Lead me to the towering rock of safety, for you are my safe refuge, a fortress where my enemies cannot reach me.

Psalms 61:1-3

Can you look at someone and determine by the clothes, hair and the body language what their story is? Do you really think that the whole story of any one person is on display and without words you have the truth about the individual? Is there a person that you have ever told everything? When you feel like you have been judged is it always comfortable to be near the person? Are you speaking from the heart and letting people know the real person, deep down, inside of you?

O LORD, you have searched me and you know me. You know when I sit and when I rise; you perceive my thoughts from afar. You discern my going out and my lying down; you are familiar with all my ways. Before a word is on my tongue you know it completely, O LORD.

Psalms 139:1-4

Yet to all who received him, to those who believed in his name, he gave the right to become children of God children born not of natural descent, nor of human decision or a husband's will, but born of God.

John 1:12-13

These scriptures tell us God knows when we sit down, when we get up, and we are His children. Do you always feel like His child? How do you feel about all of His children? Many of God's children have committed sins that would make a lot of Christians uncomfortable to be near them. We judge their actions; God judges the heart. My son has now been in jail, would you be fearful for him to sit near you? He is an addict, would that cause you to treat him unfairly? The point is.... are we sharing the gospel with "all" people? Might it be possible; we are sharing the gospel only with people we are comfortable with? Suppose this was in your church bulletin next week. Please Welcome a Well-Known Speaker: He is an Adulterer, Murderer. Failure as a Father, and a great King.

How would you feel about attending this event? Don't you know the phones lines would be very busy? Some would be very critical that the church would allow a man to stand behind the pulpit that did these kinds of things. I'm sure many of you know this is David. David, the writer of most of the Psalms was also a man after God's heart. This is the book in the Bible we turn to for strength when life is unbearable. The reason we can go through that book is because the man himself knows about pain. The reason he knows so much about pain is because he did all those things. God shows us that real men and women have real issues. But if the church would not accept David, I wonder who else we would not allow into our midst?

When the members of the Sanhedrin heard this, they were furious and gnashed their teeth at him. But Stephen, full of the Holy Spirit, looked up to heaven and saw the glory of God, and Jesus standing at the right hand of God. "Look," he said, "I see heaven open and the Son of Man standing at the right hand of God." At this they covered their ears and, yelling at the top of their voices, they all rushed at him dragged him out of the city and began to stone him. Meanwhile, the witnesses laid their coats at the feet of a young man named Saul. While they were stoning him, Stephen prayed, "Lord Jesus, receive my spirit." Then he fell on his knees and cried out, "Lord, do not hold this sin against them." When he had said this, he fell asleep.

Acts 7:54-60

This is the account of the stoning of Stephen, the heavens open up and all the people had to cover their ears because of the noise. If you notice in the scriptures, the witnesses laid their coats at the feet of a young man...his name was Saul. He watched the stoning of Stephen and approved it.

Meanwhile, Saul was still breathing out murderous threats against the Lord's disciples. He went to the high priest and asked him for letters to the synagogues in Damascus, so that if he found any there who belonged to the Way, whether men or women, he might take them as prisoners to Jerusalem. As he neared Damascus on his journey,

*suddenly a light from heaven flashed around him.
He fell to the ground and heard a voice say to him,
"Saul, Saul, why do you persecute me?" "Who are
you, Lord?" Saul asked. "I am Jesus, whom you are
persecuting," he replied. "Now get up and go into
the city, and you will be told what you must do."*

Acts 9:1-6

Saul was at the stoning of Stephen and when he was still persecuting the people of God, the Lord put a stop to him, literally! He was blinded for a time. This transformed his whole life. But in essence, murder was right there in the forefront. Do you feel change is possible? We know it is, he changed Saul and turned him into Paul the writer of most of the New Testament. Ephesians, Philippines, Colossians and Philemon were written while Paul was in prison. So do you think you would roll out the Welcome mat for Paul? Remember, he condoned murder of Christians, and he was a jail convict? I wonder if, we as Christians aren't missing something that Jesus tried so hard to tell us from the cross. Forgiveness...

*And Jesus said, "Father, forgive them, for they
know not what they do." And they cast lots to divide
his garments.*

Luke 23:34

Those soldiers were gambling for Jesus's garments, and a miraculous occurrence is taking place yet they take no notice. The Savior of the world is dying right in front of them, and they continue to live the same as they did the day before that and had not a thought in the world for the future. Jesus forgave them. We wouldn't. The only thing he owned in the world, and they are dividing it between them. Think it through.... how forgiving would you be? You may shout, just take it! But to say you have no idea what's happening, and I forgive you is not something we have inside us to offer. (Maybe you can) So are we doing it to people that we should be forgiving now? Think about people that have been able to forgive the ones that have murdered their family members, or someone who lost a child through a drunk driver, and they have stood by that person to offer support. Jesus demands that of us...He did it.

Could YOU?

15

The Lord himself goes before you and will be with you; He will never leave you nor forsake you. Do not be afraid; do not be discouraged."

Deuteronomy 31:8

The Lord goes before us, and He will never leave us! I need that reassurance many times. My grandson and I praise in the car on the way to school. God in his wonder nearly every morning will play the song that he loves. The one that speaks about, knowing who goes before me, knowing who stands behind, the God of Angel Armies is always by my side! He loves that. He knows his day will be fine, because his own Angel Army is guarding him all day. It is amazing that a little boy can understand simple scriptures that adults will talk or analyze to death.

I made a decision that will affect my son for the remainder of his life. On every application, there will be a box that he will now check because I made that phone call. I know that he caused it all, but as a parent, you want so desperately to protect your children no matter what their age. His court date is today. I know that I should go. As my little buddy and I go to school, I am very quiet and he senses, there is something wrong. He says to me.... "Gi will you pray today?" No words will come out of my mouth; my lip is trembling, and thank goodness he is in the back seat and cannot see me. After a few seconds, I clear my throat and say, "Why don't you do it?" You can't fool children. He wants to know why I'm crying. I tell him it's just one of those days, and I will be fine. His first words are… "its daddy isn't it?" He prays, and I cry. He gets out to go in the school, I tell him I love him so much and fall apart.

We listen to KLOVE each morning; on the way home they always have an encouraging story for the day. I turn the radio up and cry. I try my best to praise God. On this day, they play a song called Remember Me by Mark Schulz. If you have never heard it take time to listen, it is beautiful. I love the song, but this day I don't hear the words he is singing. When he begins to sing about remembering…I pictured my child, the first day of school. He sat down crossed his legs like the others and looked up to me and asked, "Mommy, are you really going to leave me here by myself?" I turned around and smiled, I told him he would love it. When I got into the car, I cried all the way to work. The next image in my head, he was about 7, and he had pitched in tournaments all day. He was hot and tired. We got into the car, and he reached down grabbed the "cup" (first experience it was required for tournaments) and threw it in the floorboard. He told my mother in law and me, "I will not wear that again until you sew fur on it." We laughed until we cried. The next image was my son and I in the delivery room for the birth of "his son." He was so nervous he was sick; his hands were shaking so bad he couldn't hold his girlfriend's hand. When his little boy was born, he was so proud to hold him and took him into the hall to show grandparents, aunts and uncles. I think that was the happiest I ever saw him.

It's funny how fleeting and fast images can go through the mind. By now, I am dying inside. I am pleading with God for help! I realize I cannot go to court. It was hard to see the police handcuff him, but to see my son shackled, hands and feet! I know I cannot do that. I tell God I will do whatever He asks me to do, but I beg, please don't ask that of me.

> **Near the cross of Jesus stood his mother, his mother's sister, Mary the wife of Clopas, and Mary Magdalene. When Jesus saw his mother there, and the disciple whom he loved standing nearby, he said to her, "Woman, here is your son,"**
>
> **John 19:25-26**

Please don't think in any way I would suggest the pain I experience would touch the pain Mary felt. But having gone through this it has opened my eyes to the raw emotion Mary must have been feeling. If I am suffering in the small misfortune that I have faced, what Jesus's mother was subject to cannot be explained in words. I now wonder what kept her from dying of a heart attack, or dropping upon her knees and suddenly being unable to continue breathing. I would never question it after I have been on this journey. My prayer is you never face any situation such as this.

> **Consider the blameless, observe the upright; a future awaits those who seek peace**
>
> **Psalms 37:37**

Who qualifies as blameless and upright? I know I don't. Do you? Are you a person of peace? I would love to have some peace. Right now, I feel a lot of turmoil. Even so, God does not let us operate by our feelings.

> ***But now he has reconciled you by Christ's physical
> body through death to present you holy in his sight,
> without blemish and free from accusation***
>
> > ***Colossians 1:22***

Jesus's death brought you into his presence, and you are holy and blameless as you stand before him without a single fault. When Christ died, he made us free from all the wrong things we did. Everything in your past, present and future was completely forgiven. It's free to everyone who will believe that Jesus died upon the cross and was buried and rose on the third day. It's not about how you feel. That scripture tells you that you are free from accusation, without blemish and reconciled by the death of Christ. But we spend a lot of time on how we feel, and those feelings are what lead to self-destruction.

> ***We are faithless, he remains faithful, for he cannot
> disown himself***
>
> > ***2 Timothy 2:13***

Does that help? No matter how you feel God is faithful. Feelings are fickle. You can be hot one minute, cold the next. Have you ever cried because you were happy? Explain that to men. My husband says after you have a grandchild something happens to you...you cry. That never happened to him before. His heart has become very tender, many times at night, there is a little boy in the middle of his lap telling him all kinds of things, and all that little boy would have to say is Paw-Paw, I want, and if it were within his power that little boy would get what he asks for. Now the older he gets I'm sure the wants are going to get bigger, and the no's will be much more often.

But he loves him in a much different way than he ever loved our two sons. You realize that the things that used to be important, they are not that big a deal anymore. Time is no longer just wasted; it is gone... you can never recover it. My prayer is that my grandson will grow up to be a great man of God.

> ***Then Jesus came to them and said, 'All authority in heaven and on earth has been given to me. Therefore go and make disciples of all nations, baptizing them in the name of the Father and of the Son and of the Holy Spirit, and teaching them to obey everything I have commanded you and surely I am with you always, to the very end of the age'***
>
> ***Matthew 28:18-20***

Our purpose in life is to find the good life; God has in mind for us. We have not been allowed to spend time on this earth to store up wealth and work a job that we hate. You and I as followers of Jesus are to make sure every person we come in contact with knows that Jesus died upon a cross for them, was buried and rose again. We have lots of ways to make a mess out of it. My son made choices that have affected our household drastically. He has hurt our extended family greatly. The day of court came. I did not go. Buster said he prayed and told God whatever you want I will do and understand that I deserve it. When the time came for court to start Buster was told to look around the courtroom and see if he recognized anyone. He did not. None of the officers went to court either. The judge released him with certain rules. He cannot come near me. The judge somehow thinks that I am in physical danger. They allowed him to leave on his own recognizance with a bond that matters only if he does not show back up for court, or if he disobeyed the orders. The problem is he has nowhere to go. Remember, when I said family wanted information, but would not help, that is the case. My mother is considering allowing him to stay with her. I have been completely honest with her, and she knows the truth about his lies, addictions and the arrest. She has been up all night and can't come to a conclusion. He has been in our home, and cannot sleep...fearful all the time the police will come back and arrest him for not complying with the order of the bond. He must have a new address in two days to give to his probation officer. He thinks he has a job. This will be the first in five years. He dozes from exhaustion but cannot relax to sleep. I am praying almost constantly, but half the time I have no idea what to even ask God for.

My mother made the decision to allow Buster to come and live with her, since the court order stated he could have no contact with me. (Mother) He and his grandmother had a conversation stating the rules he would need to follow while living at her home. She lives within five miles from our home in another city. It is smaller and Buster knows no one. Everyday Buster rides into the city he is familiar with and stays all day and rides back to my mothers in the afternoon. Buster insisted this whole time he was drug free. He said he was going for drug screens with probation officer and had not failed at any time. Addicts lie! They will say just about anything to anyone to keep getting the drugs their body craves.

This situation has continued for some time and again it has caused another problem with more family. This time it runs deeper. God will have to repair the damage done this time, no words that I could ever offer would help. I have received text messages; phone calls and one time a visit at home so that a person could voice their disgust of Buster and of me. At no time, have I offered any explanation. Anger out of control would never repair damage that has already taken place. No explanation I could offer would be enough for someone who has decided they have the answer. My mistakes are many, and I admit to them all the time. Buster made his own choice, and I did not cause his addiction in any way. However, when other people try to hurt and blame you, the pain can become so great you can be overwhelmed to the point you cannot even convey your thoughts and feelings.

After some time, (it felt like months) Buster went back to court and was sent to jail. He was absolutely miserable. He called begging for money...how is it possible he still wants money even in jail? This money is for the phone and for commissary. This is a real money trap but his child cannot talk to him at all, and again I feel like I would be doing the wrong thing not allowing his son the ability to talk with his dad...

After eighty-one days, Buster has his court date. This time I go and when he comes into the room, he is shackled, and I had to look away. Some people may find this amusing. However, I have never seen my child in this condition and have no prior experience within the justice system. Buster has been accepted by a rehabilitation center in another state. The judge wants no part of this and is quick to state this will not happen. After a couple of hours, his attorney and the Assistant District Attorney work together, and present before the judge a new option and finally the judge accepts the proposal, but it is with great skepticism. He reminds Buster about the amount of confidence that has been placed in him by these people, and if he fails he could face additional jail time. Buster assures him that he completely understands. The judge demands that Buster be transported the same day to the new location.

The three of us, Buster, his Dad and I leave at 5:30 and drive for nine hours. Buster finally tells us that it was in jail that he ultimately got free of the drugs. His blood pressure got so low at one point; the medical staff at the jail thought they would have to transport him to the hospital. He was very sick for days. Praise God he is finally drug free. He is looking forward to the chance for a new start, but does fear the chance of failure.

I would be overly concerned if he knew that he would be fine. He is going into a city and state he has never been. He will be involved in Christian counseling. He is required by the court to be back in jail in exactly six months. He has six months to change half a lifetime of habits that he cannot explain. Buster wants answers. He wants to know why he is this person. He wants to be sure he never goes back to that lifestyle.

> *In the same way, the Spirit helps us in our weakness.*
> *We do not know what we ought to pray for, but the*
> *Spirit himself intercedes for us through wordless*
> *groans*
>
> **Romans 8:26**

Aren't you thankful for a God that understands! When I don't even know what to pray for, and when I moan the Spirit is well aware of the weakness that I feel right now. He intercedes for me, because I truly am in a position of hopelessness. Not with God! Never Him! God gives us chances over and over. It's a refining process. Like precious metals are melted in fire, they are molded into beautiful jewels that have high value. We are the same way to God. We are in the fire sometimes, and sometimes we are being molded, but when we belong to Him, the value is priceless. This is walking by faith. You must recognize that you will face a time to walk in darkness by faith. The purpose throughout this book is hopefully to keep you from this situation to begin with.

I would love to tell you ......and they lived happily ever after. I cannot. That is in fairy tales. This is real life. I want so desperately to tell you that I love Buster unconditionally, but I can't. I am so hurt. The child I remember and the man he has become are not the one I had hoped he would be. I am so glad God never gives up on me. If you are disappointed to hear me say this, you can't feel any worse than I do. God is showing me once again, how much He has to put up with me. I have failed Him so very much.

This is knowledge and with knowledge comes responsibilities. You and I must do something to help put a stop to this destruction of our children. Get very involved in your child's life. Remember, I do a lot of Beth Moore s Bible Studies. One that forever changed my life was the study of James. The reason is the same in our homes today. Jesus half-brothers were not aware of who Jesus was. They were sharing a room at night (most likely) with Jesus and had no idea he was the Messiah.

> ***Then Jesus entered a house, and again a crowd gathered, so that he and his disciples were not even able to eat. When his family heard about this, they went to take charge of him, for they said, "He is out of his mind."***
>
> ***Mark 3:20-21***

His family at this point came to get him because they thought he was losing his mind. Jesus own brothers, maybe sisters, we don't know who was there. But we do know this is fact because it is in the Word of God. So how did James, change his mind?

> *For what I received I passed on to you as of first importance: that Christ died for our sins according to the Scriptures, that he was buried, that he was raised on the third day according to the Scriptures, and that he appeared to Cephas, and then to the Twelve. After that, he appeared to more than five hundred of the brothers and sisters at the same time, most of whom are still living, though some have fallen asleep. Then he appeared to James, then to all the apostles, and last of all he appeared to me also, as to one abnormally born.*
>
> *1 Corinthians 15: 3-8*

Read those scriptures. It tells us he appeared to James. His brother who at one time thought he was crazy. I think that is so important. James grew up without the truth, even though he was closer to it than anyone, Jesus loved him and gave him respect by appearing to him before the apostles. Do you wonder what they said to each other? Was it brother to brother or Savior to a lost soul that just found out he was not going to die and be separated from the "brother" we all have? Did they hug and cry? What if you are like James…you get close enough to talk about it and see it but not close enough to go and be part of the family?

> *Then after three years, I went up to Jerusalem to get acquainted with Cephas and stayed with him fifteen days. I saw none of the other apostles—only*

> ***James, the Lord's brother. I assure you before God***
> ***that what I am writing you is no lie.***
>
> ***Galatians 1:18-20***

These are Paul's writings; he was not one of the twelve apostles. He wanted to spend time with Peter and again in scriptures you see again James is mentioned. This is after the resurrection. James was given a second chance. We all are given additional chances while we are here on this earth. God loves us so much he gave us His only Son. That is more love than we are capable of giving to another person. Only God can love that much.

I heard a story today, and it tears at my heart...I will tell it this way. Suppose Madonna was invited to sing at a wedding. It was a special event. It was at the White House. Suppose the person taking the tickets was eighty-one, never watched TV or listened to radio. She has been instructed; no one enters this party, unless they have the confirmation from the White House. Madonna arrives, but she was far too busy to call back to confirm the date and reservation. She explains to the lady at the door who she is, how important she is and how much money she has, but none of that matters. Without the ticket, she will not let her in. That is how Heaven will be. We get our ticket here. We cannot get the ticket at the gate. We can't talk our way in, buy our way in or pay our way in. Some people think they have a ticket, but sadly they do not. Do you? Have you been too busy to take time and attend to things that are very important? Do you really know what is going on in your own home and with your children? Pray for our nation, we have lost our commitment to God. Family is no longer important, and that is how things have gotten so out of control. When we removed God from school, we lost our morals and the children have no values for their lives.

God is the answer for whatever your problem is, you can overcome anything. He will help you, and you will never be alone again. You will not be problem free, but you will know how to deal with your problems. You will know that your future is secure, and you will know that you are LOVED.

Epilogue

As of the print of Desperate Destruction, Buster is in rehabilitation and very happy. He has Bible Study from 5:00 to 9:00 in the morning. His first job was at a car wash. He has graduated to painting, and hopes to get promoted to the grounds keeping job. (He worked at the golf course when his little boy was born and loved it) After work, there is more Bible Study. He is amazed that he is receiving this much study! He loves it. He is not completely surrounded by honorable people, but he has identified the troublemakers and stayed away from them.

The true test will be when Buster returns to this city. Can he confront and oppose the temptation? I cannot do this for him, but my prayers are that he will be strong enough now to walk away from that kind of life. Time will tell.

CPSIA information can be obtained at www.ICGtesting.com
Printed in the USA
LVOW09s0846191114

414292LV00002B/3/P